Pruning Trees, Shrubs & Vines

Janet Marinelli
SERIES EDITOR

Sigrun Wolff Saphire
SENIOR EDITOR

Mark C. Tebbitt
SCIENCE EDITOR

Tricia Chambers
ART DIRECTOR

Joni Blackburn
COPY EDITOR

Chris Roddick
CONSULTING ARBORIST

Steven Clemants
VICE-PRESIDENT,
SCIENCE & PUBLICATIONS

Judith D. Zuk
PRESIDENT

Elizabeth Scholtz
DIRECTOR EMERITUS

Cover: Pruning a rosebush. Above: *Daphne* × *burkwoodii,* **a small shrub.**

Pruning Trees, Shrubs & Vines

By Karan Davis Cutler

Handbook #176

Copyright © 2003 by Brooklyn Botanic Garden, Inc.

All-Region Guides, formerly *21st-Century Gardening Series,* are published three times a year at 1000 Washington Ave., Brooklyn, NY 11225.

Subscription included in Brooklyn Botanic Garden subscriber membership dues ($35 per year; $45 outside the United States).

ISBN # 1-889538-59-0

Printed by Science Press, a division of the Mack Printing Group. Printed on recycled paper.

Pruning Trees, Shrubs & Vines
Table of Contents

The Why and When of Pruning 6

The Kindest Cuts: Where and How to Prune .18

Shrubs: Pruning the Workhorses of the Garden 28

Deciduous Trees: Pruning the Garden's Monuments 40

Conifers: Pruning Coniferous Trees and Shrubs 54

Vines and Climbers: Pruning Plants That Ascend 66

Roses: Pruning the Sweetest Flower 76

Special Cases: Pruning for Particular Purposes 88

Outfitting the Pruner: Tools and Equipment 100

For More Information 110

Organizations and Suppliers 111

Contributors 113

Index 114

Opposite: If you love giving your pruners a real workout, topiary is for you. Popular since Roman times, this pruning technique requires time, patience, a good eye, and suitable small-leafed plants that don't mind constant snipping.

The Why and When of Pruning

Down the road from me is a sugarhouse that neighbors long ago abandoned. It is encased in Boston ivy (*Parthenocissus tricuspidata*). Left to its own devices, the vine has wound and wrapped and crisscrossed and crept until the shack has disappeared. What's left is a sugarhouse made solely of leaves, green in summer and maroon in autumn. Only in winter are the supporting wood walls and slate roof visible.

Every time I pass I am reminded of the delicious description by the French novelist Colette of the exuberant but sinister *Wisteria* that grew on the garden walls where she was born (*Flowers and Fruit,* 1986). As she sits in her former home, the wisteria strikes:

> The sudden shattering of a windowpane made me shudder, and decided it: a vegetable arm, crooked, twisted, in which I had no difficulty recognizing the workings, the surreptitious approach, the reptilian mind of the wisteria, had just struck, broken, and entered.

That's what happens when you leave some plants to their own devices. Gardeners soon learn that they must exercise a bit of authority over what they grow. What Colette—and my neighbors—needed was a pair of sharp

Good pruning is like good acting: It is invisible.

Opposite: Size matters. Think way ahead when you buy plants and be sure to choose species or cultivars that match the available space. Live oak, *Quercus virginiana,* may grow to 80 feet tall.

Allow plants such as *Forsythia*, above, to grow into their natural shapes, pruning mostly to encourage flowering and to eliminate the oldest stems. Plants pruned only as needed will look their best.

pruning shears. Every gardener needs a pair, and a pruning saw as well.

Nature has its own ways of keeping plants in check. Fire reorders landscapes for decades, sometimes forever. Competition between plants allows the stronger and taller and longer-lived to conquer or hamper the weaker and smaller and fugacious. Shallow-rooted trees topple when the ground becomes saturated from rain, while leaders—the main, or terminal, shoots—die back when there is too little moisture. Limbs bend under the weight of ice and break in high winds. Diseases and insects take their toll, as do larger animals: elk, moose, porcupines, beavers, rabbits, mice, birds, and white-tail deer, the plant pruners par excellence in my region of New England.

It's our bad luck that nature doesn't always do what we want, especially on small city and suburban lots. I live on 15 wooded acres and have room to let most things grow as they will, but I don't want the climbing hydrangea (*Hydrangea petiolaris*) to shroud the guest-room windows, nor do I want the red maples (*Acer rubrum*) to shade out the tree lilac (*Syringa reticulata*). I do want the summersweet (*Clethra alnifolia*) by my patio to stay small and compact, and I'd like flowers covering the entire 'Comtesse de Bouchaud' clematis in my atrium, not just the top four feet. California friends treasure their marbled bamboo hedge (*Chimonobambusa marmorea*), but they don't want it to take over their yard.

Many gardeners never think about training or cutting back plants until the neighbor is bleeding from a head-to-limb encounter with the crabapple (*Malus*) someone planted too close to a path or it's impossible to get past the eastern white pine (*Pinus strobus*) and through the front door. These are pruning SOSs. Reminders, too, that many pruning jobs are avoided if you choose the right plant for the site.

Beginning a new garden? Do yourself a favor and think *waaay* ahead when buying woody plants. Those five-foot blue spruces that perfectly frame the front door now can't be kept that small forever. Boston ivy won't just cover a wall, it will cover the neighborhood. Rhododendrons the size of laundry baskets get to be the size of garden sheds. Like the national debt, most plants just keep getting bigger. If you must prune a plant drastically once or twice a year to make it fit its spot, it's the wrong plant—or the right plant in the wrong spot.

Gardeners with zillions of acres who want shade can plant a pin oak. But if you have a small yard and also want to grow cosmos and Shasta daisies, *Quercus palustris* isn't for you. The happy news is that your choices aren't wholly limited just because your acreage is pinched. Breeders have been busy miniaturizing just about every species

Left: Eastern arborvitae, *Thuja occidentalis* 'Rheingold', is a small cultivar, easily kept in bounds with minimal pruning. If you prune beautybush, *Kolkwitzia amabilis,* seen above the arborvitae, it won't flower. Right: Winterberry, *Ilex verticillata,* does best with little pruning.

Left: When two branches rub against each other, one needs to be removed. Right: Remove a broken branch as soon as you notice it.

known to humankind, as well as grafting standards on dwarfing rootstocks to keep them small. We gardeners, to paraphrase slightly, can have our plants and keep them too.

But if there is a huge and spectacularly fragrant *Syringa vulgaris* growing too close to the back door and you can't bear cutting it down, there is still a solution. Pruning. Bonsai—which involves grooming a woody plant that would normally tower over the gardener to be 11 inches tall and look as if it predated Moses—is as much art as craft, but everyday pruning can be learned. And put an accent on "everyday." I once lived in a house owned by a small midwestern college. That college's approach—carried out just before the alumni and parents arrived for commencement—was to top every shrub and vine and remove all dangling tree limbs. Come May, anything green between 4 feet and 15 feet off the ground was history. English garden writer David Joyce calls this the "vague notion that at some time in the year all plants need to be tidied up."

Examples of dreadful pruning are everywhere: You have only to look under the power lines of any city to explain why so many of us are timid about taking a sharp blade to a plant we have spent years encouraging to grow. But any gardener can learn to prune properly. The secret is that pruning must be *planned* and *ongoing*. The outcome is that anyone looking at your work won't see it. Good pruning is like good acting: It is invisible.

The Reasons Why

Pruning is removing parts of a plant, either above or below ground. Training, an associative term, usually refers to shaping a plant to a desired form. Gardeners prune and train to ensure safety; to maintain a plant's good health; to limit or promote growth; to shape; to encourage flowering and fruiting; and to renew and repair. Put more simply, you prune to keep yourself safe, to keep plants hale and hearty, and to make them do—as far as humanly possible and sensible—what you want them to do. Don't assume that frequent pruning is necessary for every woody plant in your landscape. Desultory pruning is a mistake too. Always know why you're sawing, snipping, and shearing.

Pruning for Safety Making sure woody plants don't injure people or structures should be the first item on anyone's pruning agenda. Pruning for safety includes removing branches that threaten to fall and do damage; trimming limbs that may interfere with utility lines; cutting back growth that blocks the line of sight at driveway and street intersections; curbing thorny plants that endanger passersby; lightening vines that threaten to bring down trellises and other supports; and taming plants that are growing into someone else's yard. In addition to protecting yourself and your family, the objective is to be a good neighbor. And to avoid being sued.

Pruning for Good Health For good health, begin with the two D's: Prune wood that is damaged or dead; it always needs to come off. Also remove branches that rub against each other, as well as branches with weak, unnatural branch-union angles, as they are vulnerable to breaking. Remove suckers and thin out *water sprouts,* or *epicormic shoots,* which are weakly attached vertical shoots that emerge from latent buds.

Pruning to Limit Growth Owners of Lilliputian lots have a special interest in hogtying plants. The math is simple: Smaller equals more. One standard pear tree dominates a tiny garden, but espalier that tree—train it against a vertical surface—and there is space left for a spicebush (*Lindera benzoin*) and a firethorn (*Pyracantha coccinea*), and you'll still have fresh pears for the picking.

Everyone who gardens will want to constrain something sometime. Most species are cooperative *if* you don't wait until they are shading the roof of your house or have secondary limbs the size of a boxer's neck. Eastern arborvitae (*Thuja occidentalis*), for instance, stretches to 50 feet on its own, but you can keep it at 5 feet or reduce its girth if that's what will safeguard your view of the mountains. If cooling a plant's size is the aim, follow the country wisdom: "Weak growth, prune hard; strong growth, prune light."

That adage comes from the ostensibly illogical fact that pruning can stimulate growth, especially severe pruning undertaken in early spring. Cut back a healthy main shoot, and it will sprout secondary shoots. (More about this below.) Pruning can be a way to promote growth as well as to curb it.

Pruning to Shape The last word in plant shaping is topiary—an art invented some 2,000 years ago by the Romans—but even gardeners who don't want boxwood peacocks and yew sheep grazing on their lawn may have an interest in tailoring their plants. Most of the work can be done with hand pruners, and the usual goal is aesthetic.

Unless you yearn for green obelisks to frame the front door or you're maintaining a hedge, it's smart to follow the plant's lead. Most species are inherently graceful. *Forsythia,* for example, is far more beautiful when just the old stems are removed and the remaining stems are allowed to cascade freely than when it's cut back severely. Different shrubs and trees have distinct forms. Trying to change those natural patterns, especially with large trees, is a time-consuming and often frustrating undertaking.

You may want to prune off low limbs to reveal attractive bark or interesting stem and trunk forms—a technique called *lifting*—or remove errant shoots, or shear a conifer to encourage symmetry. And pruning and shaping doesn't have to mean artificial. Japanese gardens are the epitome of controlled growth: Every tree and shrub is painstakingly trimmed in order to appear natural. Trees with gardener-encouraged multistem trunks or asymmetrical shapes may be exactly what your "natural" landscape needs.

Pruning to Encourage Flowering and Fruiting Pruning is a fundamental tool of fruit growers, who shape and control their trees to enhance their crops. But pruning shouldn't be left to the orchardists. Flowers and fruits (as well as leaves and stems) are important in the ornamental garden. Their colors, size, and number can be enhanced by strategic pruning.

For example, pruning young plants stimulates vegetative growth and delays the production of flowers and fruits. Rosarians who want jumbo blooms for the annual garden show prune their plants heavily, but they do less cutting back if more flowers is the goal. Fruit-bearing ornamental shrubs, such as winterberry (*Ilex verticillata*), American cranberry bush (*Viburnum trilobum*), and *Rosa rugosa,* bear more fruits if pruned only lightly or not at all.

Many gardeners regularly cut back *Kerria japonica,* red osier and Tartarian dogwoods (*Cornus stolonifera, C. alba*), and other shrubs grown for their brightly hued stems to promote new shoots, which are more intensely colored than older ones. Leaf color of other plants, such as purple-leafed filbert (*Corylus maxima* 'Purpurea') and redtip (*Photinia* × *fraseri*), can be augmented if not magnified by well-timed pruning.

Pruning to Repair or Renew Repairing or renewing a mature plant can be ugly—there's no instant gratification in this kind of pruning. But when a tree, shrub, or vine is damaged or allowed to outgrow its space, drastic surgery may be required. Severe pruning, which may mean topping (removing most or all of a plant's crown) or cutting plants to the ground, carries risks. Some species grow back successfully, but others, such as arborvitae, cedar, juniper, pine, and other conifers, respond less successfully—or not at all. If a mature tree needs to be topped, remove it instead.

To promote an abundance of intensely colored new shoots, many gardeners regularly cut back shrubs grown for their brightly hued stems, such as red osier dogwood, *Cornus stolonifera*.

Before the First Cut

A southern California cousin of mine was surprised to learn that Vermonters don't set out tomatoes in March. Climate doesn't only affect when gardeners plant, it affects how and when we prune. Trees in warm, humid regions need open canopies; in hot, arid conditions, heavy, compact growth is an asset, not a liability. In some parts of the country, late winter means February, in others April. Like politics, all gardening is local, so consult neighborhood gardeners, local growers, nursery owners, and other authorities for advice about when to prune.

It's also important to know something about how plants grow before you head for the garden armed with loppers and saw. In a nutshell, pruning affects plants' size and the way they grow, and it alters their carbohydrate-to-nitrogen ratio.

Size reduction seems straightforward enough: You remove growth and the plant is smaller. But it's not quite that easy, for pruning also stimulates growth. Confusing, yes, but the bottom line is that pruning, done correctly, yields a plant smaller than it was before you pruned.

All new growth comes from buds. Plants grow up and out from the tips of their shoots. Woody species, the subject of this book, have *lateral,* or *auxiliary,* buds that are arranged along branches in different ways—either opposite or alternate—depending on the plant. These buds, which arise where leaves attach, at nodes, are separated by sections of branch called *internodes.* Woody plants also have latent buds, less visible dormant buds that lie under the bark.

Both lateral and latent buds take their growing orders from the apical, or terminal, bud that is located at the tip of the branch. Apical buds produce auxins, hormones that suppress the growth of the lateral buds below the tip, an effect botanists call *apical dominance.* Cut off the apical bud, which stops the production of auxins, and the lateral and latent buds closest to the cut are signaled to grow. (In addition to affecting lateral bud break, apical dominance also influences the length of lateral shoots and the angle at which they are joined to the limb.)

The potency of apical dominance not only varies from one species to another but is influenced by orientation: Lateral buds on horizontal branches are less restrained by the apical bud, while lateral buds on vertical growth are strongly suppressed. Train a crabapple's limb to grow horizontally, remove the apical bud, and the lateral buds will erupt in water sprouts that you'll need to remove. Age, too, has an effect. Apical dominance is pronounced in young plants but less strong in older plants, which is why many conifers lose their Christmas-tree shape and develop rounded crowns when they mature. Similarly, if you head back a year-old stem, the effect on the lateral buds is more pronounced than if you head back a branch that is ten years old.

Finally, the vigor of the new growth is also influenced by where you cut. The farther back you cut a shoot, the more robust the new growth. (The plant is attempting to keep its root system in balance by regrowing its top.) Pinch out the growing tip of a stem and the effect is modest; cut back a shoot by two thirds and the result is an onslaught of sprouting lateral buds.

Pruning a plant also changes its carbohydrate-nitrogen balance. Removing vegetative growth reduces both stored carbohydrates and their manufacture (carbohydrates are produced in the leaves). As a result, the higher level of nitrogen in the plant stimulates vegetative growth at the expense of reproductive growth. So pruning usually means more shoots and leaves and fewer flowers and fruits. Severe pruning, especially of young plants, can mean no flowers and fruits for several years. (Alternatively, root pruning lowers the nitrogen level and encourages both root and reproductive growth, as nutrients, including nitrogen, are taken up by the roots.)

This boxwood, *Buxus*, hedge was leggy and overgrown and needed to be pruned back to 8 to 12 inches. If you check plants regularly for their pruning needs and attend to them, you'll be able to avoid drastic measures in most cases.

When to Cut

The traditional wisdom, "Prune when the knife is sharp," is only good advice part of the time. You can prune any time of year without killing your plants, but you may weaken them if you do so over and over again. For some woody plants, when you scissor and saw isn't crucial, but that isn't true for many species, especially if flowers or fruits are your aim. If you want to realize your plants' "ornamental potential," as current gardenspeak puts it, you need to prune at the appropriate time.

Right now is always the best time to remove dead or damaged wood. Responding quickly reduces the chance of more difficulties later. And don't wait to remove growth that is dangerous or poses a liability, such as a large limb that threatens to fall on your neighbor's new Jaguar XK8 convertible. Don't delay pruning new shrubs to eliminate crossing branches, multiple central leaders, and other structural problems. But let newly planted trees grow for at least a year before you prune.

In tropical zones like those of southern Florida and southern California, gardeners prune throughout the year (although even there it's a good idea to observe plants' growth cycles). For the rest of us, residents of temperate climates, the "when" of pruning is consequential. The worst time to prune is in spring immediately after new growth has developed, because you're removing the foliage that is replenishing the plant's food supply.

The late dormant season—just before new growth begins—is the best time for pruning most woody plants. With exceptions, of course. Severely cut back a lilac (*Syringa*) or an American cranberry bush (*Viburnum trilobum*) in late winter, and

Having outgrown their space, these evergreens are now obscuring the windows. With smaller cultivars this problem could have been avoided.

come late spring there will be few blossoms to enjoy. Pruning flowering species at the correct time of year is especially important.

Fall is prime pruning time for gardeners who have very mild winters. Since cutting back promotes growth, cold-climate gardeners should limit their autumn pruning to avoid winterkill.

Winter, specifically late winter when days begin to lengthen but before new growth begins, is the time to prune summer-flowering plants that set buds on new growth in spring, such as *Camellia,* crape myrtles (*Lagerstroemia*), goldenrain tree (*Koelreuteria paniculata*), and mimosa (*Albizia julibrissin*). This is also the time for much general pruning and for renewal pruning, as new growth is only weeks away and wounds will be exposed only a short time before they seal. In some tree species like maples (*Acer*) and birches (*Betula*), sap will flow, but this is normal and not harmful to the tree, provided that pruning cuts are made correctly. (Another option is to prune these trees in late summer, when less sap will be lost.) Late winter, when leaves are down, is the easiest time to evaluate the "framework" of deciduous shrubs and trees that may need reshaping.

Spring, after growth begins, is an acceptable time to cut out damaged or dead wood; to remove small shoots heading in the wrong direction; to pinch back new growth; and to shear conifer hedges. In general, pruning in late spring strains deciduous plants and is not recommended.

Summer—early summer—is the time to prune spring-flowering plants that set buds the previous fall and have just finished blooming. Crabapples (*Malus*), *Forsythia,* lilacs (*Syringa*), and *Wisteria* are prominent examples. Because new growth slows in late summer, that's also a good time to remove suckers and thin out water sprouts, to trim hedges, to basal-prune evergreens, to pinch back stems after flowering, and to prune trees that have outgrown their location.

Avoid pruning plants when they are especially open to attacks by insects or diseases. Oaks, for instance, are vulnerable to oak wilt if they are pruned before late summer; plants susceptible to fire blight, such as apples and flowering crabapples (*Malus*), pears (*Pyrus*), mountain ash (*Sorbus aucuparia*), hawthorns (*Crataegus*), and *Spiraea,* should not be pruned in spring or summer, or during warm, humid conditions when fire blight spreads freely. There's always less chance of transmitting diseases if you prune when the weather is dry rather than when it's wet.

Maybe a rose is a rose is a rose, but you can't assume that all cultivars of the same species can be pruned at the same time or the same way. Some *Clematis* cultivars flower on the current season's growth, or *new wood*; other cultivars flower on *old wood,* shoots produced the previous year; and still others flower on both old and new wood. Each group is pruned differently. Generalizations are helpful, but generalizations are not particulars. No single rule works for all plants.

Pruning Roots

In addition to growing up from the tips of their stems, plants grow down (and out) from the tips of their roots. Root pruning, which removes many of those tips, reduces a plant's water and nutrient uptake, changes its carbohydrate-nitrogen balance, and slows its growth.

Exposed roots of healthy, young shrubs and trees can be removed. If you're worried about how much root to cut off, err on the side of caution. Girdling roots, roots that wrap around the base of a young plant, should be removed as soon as you detect them. Never remove large girdling roots of mature trees.

Root pruning—slicing into the soil with a spade at the plant's drip line—is one way to slow growth and is often used to prepare field plants for transplanting. The technique is more effective with shrubs and vines than with trees, although espaliered trees respond to root pruning.

Remember the Risks

While many species are altogether forgiving, sawing and slicing always carries some risk, especially severe sawing and slicing. The best way to minimize the dangers is to prune at the correct time and in the correct way. The golden rule of pruning is, "When in doubt, don't." Many trees, shrubs, and vines do fine without interference. Too much pruning may destroy their natural grace. Palms, rhododendrons, magnolias, and many conifers, such as Norfolk Island pines (*Araucaria heterophylla*), are just a few plants that should be approached carefully. If you've placed them where they have room to spread, leave them alone except for maintenance pruning and a shaping cut here and there.

The Kindest Cuts:
Where and How to Prune

Even if you're not interested in becoming a pruning virtuoso, you don't want to be a botanical butcher. Any pruning stresses trees, shrubs, and vines—it's surgery, after all. A faultily pruned plant won't recover for years. Perhaps never. At the least, you need to know how to achieve your pruning objectives while doing as little harm as possible.

A faultily pruned plant won't recover for years. Perhaps never.

The term "pruning" has come to mean everything from cutting, pinching, delimbing, heading, and shaping to trimming, disbudding, topping, shearing, thinning, and more. Whatever the method—or the term—the pruner's aim is to keep people and property safe, and to keep plants healthy, productive, attractive, and in bounds. Over time you'll develop your own pruning techniques, but it never hurts to take advantage of others' knowledge and experience. No need to reinvent the pruning wheel.

However small or large the job—and whatever your goal—for the health of the plant:

- Unless it's a topiary or hedge, respect the natural form of the plant when you prune. Don't overstress plants by cutting away too much at one time. Always cut back to healthy, living wood.

Opposite: The goal of pruning is to keep plants healthy, productive, attractive, and in bounds. Rhododendrons require little pruning beyond deadheading and removing very old wood.

A peach tree pruned to create an open framework.

- Make clean cuts. No ragged edges, no torn or bruised bark.
- No hat pegs, as the British say. That means don't leave stubs and snags when you cut and saw.
- Don't expect pruning to solve problems created by an inadequate site or poor maintenance.

And for your own health, use the proper tools, wear safety gear, know where limbs will fall, count your fingers, and keep your ladder upright.

Heading Cuts and Thinning Cuts

If you're a novice gardener, the place to start is with understanding the differences between and the effects of heading and thinning. All pruning begins with these two basic approaches.

Heading or *heading back,* is cutting off a portion of a stem or branch. Since heading eliminates the terminal bud, it forces new growth close beneath the cut. (See "The Why and When of Pruning," page 6, for more on the effects of removing terminal buds.) The more stem you remove, the more vigorous the new growth on the portion that's left. If you want to invigorate a plant, to encourage branching and bushiness, heading back shoots and limbs is the way to do it. Heading back, which is also known as *tipping,* is most effective with young stems.

When heading, make your cuts above a node—the point on the stem where buds, leaves, or stems are attached. Now the bud or buds just below the cut become the stem's new growing point, or terminal. Heading causes especially dense regrowth in maples (*Acer*), lilacs (*Syringa*), *Clematis,* and other plants with *opposite* buds,

Alternate and Opposite Buds

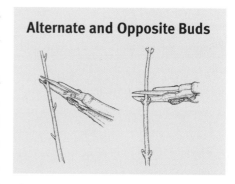

Always make a heading cut right above a bud: On a plant with alternate buds (left), angle the cut away from the bud; on a plant with opposite buds (right), cut straight across the stem.

Heading and Thinning Cuts

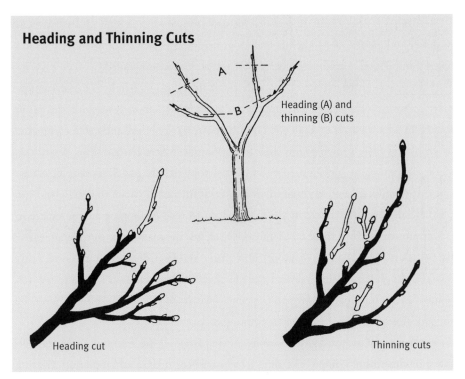

Heading (A) and thinning (B) cuts

Heading cut

Thinning cuts

Heading is cutting off a portion of a stem. It eliminates the terminal bud, forcing new growth below the cut. Thinning is removing an entire stem or branch. It produces less regrowth.

species with leaves that appear in pairs at each node, one on each side of the stem. That's because both buds form new growth. As a result, most woody plants with opposite buds tend to have a rounded shape, or at least a rounded crown.

On birches (*Betula*), roses (*Rosa*), passionflowers (*Passiflora*), and other plants with *alternate* foliage—one bud per node—heading back produces less branching but guides the direction of new growth. Cut to an outside bud—one pointing away from the center of the plant—and the new shoot heads in an outward direction; cut to an inside bud, and the new shoot grows in an inward direction. You'll want new stems heading out, which encourages an open habit and permits more sun and air to reach the inside of the plant. Unless there is a real need to "fill in" a plant's center, always cut to an outward bud.

Heading also affects flowering and fruiting because it alters the balance between above- and below-ground growth. The more stems and leaves you remove, the harder the plant tries to replace them—at the expense of flowers and fruits. Heading a young plant, especially, delays the development of flowers and fruits. Prune a mature plant lightly and blooms will be plentiful, but each will be smaller; prune severely and flowers and fruits will be larger but fewer in number.

Heading was once standard practice for new trees, shrubs, or vines. Now that most nurseries and garden centers sell container-grown plants—which don't suffer root loss when transplanted—heading is not needed and is not recommended.

Heading the entire crown of a woody plant to reduce its height is known as *topping, stubbing,* or *lopping.* The approach, also called *hat racking* since the result resembles a hat rack, is used all too often by power, telephone, and cable companies to keep trees from growing into their lines. Garden writer Barbara Ellis describes a victim of topping as "a disfigured tree with a canopy of stumps." Trees that have been topped are unlikely ever to regain their natural form and are open to disease and sun scald. Their new growth will be thick but weak. Instead of topping a tree, replace it.

Topping overgrown shrubs and vines also stresses the plants, but sometimes it may be necessary—and can have more satisfactory results. Most vines respond fairly quickly, but plan on waiting several years for established deciduous shrubs to recover. Some—including many evergreen species—won't recover and should never be topped. Always think of topping as pruning of last resort.

Another form of heading is *shearing,* cutting back all the stems of a plant to follow a predetermined shape. Customarily reserved for hedges and topiaries, shearing works well with some species, such as boxwood (*Buxus*) and yew (*Taxus*), but would be disastrous—and possibly lethal—with a *Rhododendron.* (For more on shearing, see "Special Cases," page 88.)

The easiest, safest, and most effective form of heading is *pinching,* using your thumb and index finger to nip out the tender growing tip of a shoot. No tools are required, wounds are small and close up quickly, and the plant doesn't look as if it has been scalped. Pinching slows growth—it's an effective tool for keeping plants small—and is virtually imperceptible.

Using proper technique will help avoid most pruning accidents, such as tearing off bark.

Thinning is removing an entire shoot, stem, or branch back to its point of origin, the main stem, a lateral stem, or even to the ground. Thinning opens woody plants, promoting good health by reducing foliage and allowing more air and light to reach their interiors. It is less invigorating than heading, produces less regrowth, and better allows plants to retain their natural forms.

Left: The lower branches of this paperbark maple, *Acer griseum*, were removed to reveal the bark. Right: A victim of topping, this tree will not recover its grace and may die.

Thinning cuts are also used on woody plants to establish strong frameworks and to direct and shape growth.

Crown thinning, which is most commonly used when pruning deciduous trees, is the selective removal of center growth in the crown, or canopy, while maintaining the plant's natural form. Reducing the density of the crown and correcting asymmetrical growth are the usual reasons for crown thinning. *Crown raising*—also called *lifting* or *skirting*—refers to removing branches at the bottom of a plant, cutting back to the main stems or trunk.

Raising the crown may be a way to keep a plant that has overgrown its site—a pair of 40-foot Norway spruces (*Picea abies*) planted by the front door, for example—or the solution to the nothing-will-grow problem under the stately American beech (*Fagus grandifolia*) in the front yard. Raising the crown can open the view, reduce shade, and make plants more attractive. It isn't always an ideal solution—some plants, conifers in particular, look awkward without their bottom limbs, but lifting may be a better alternative than having to cut down a mature tree, shrub, or vine.

Renewal pruning of plants also involves thinning cuts, lots of them. Trees with a single trunk—and plants that have been grafted—are thinned of everything except the limbs you want to retain as the basic framework. Multistemmed plants can be renewed by cutting the stems to the ground, either all at once or over several seasons.

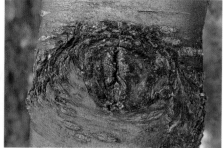

Left: A tree is forming woundwood around the perimeter of a proper pruning cut.
Right: Eventually, the tree will close off the wound completely.

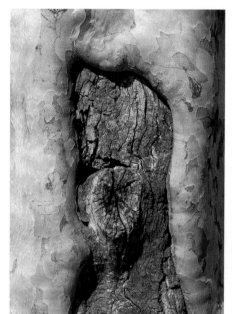

Left and right: If the bark on the trunk or the branch collar are injured when a branch is removed, the tree cannot form woundwood properly and is open to infection by pathogens.

Know as much as you can about a plant's habit—how it grows, how it responds to pruning—before you attempt renewal pruning. Renewal pruning is a grievous shock to all woody plants, and they don't all respond the same way. Some species, such as mountain laurel (*Kalmia latifolia*) and many conifers, are famously intolerant of such manhandling. Even plants that ought to respond well to renewal pruning sometimes don't. I've cut a European cranberry bush (*Viburnum opulus*) to the ground a half-dozen times and it still comes back, but renewal pruning was lethal to my doublefile viburnum (*Viburnum plicatum* f. *tomentosum*). Renewing sometimes means replacing.

Making the Cut

Before you rip into pruning your trees, shrubs, and vines, have the appropriate tools and be sure that they are sharp and in good repair. Hand pruners are made for small cuts, loppers and pruning saws for bigger jobs, and pole pruners and saws for limbs you can't reach from the ground. (There is more about tools in "Outfitting the Pruner," page 100.) Most pruning cuts are pretty straightforward, but there are a few tricks you should know.

Small Cuts For jobs that can be done easily with pruning shears—cutting shoots, stems, and branches less than one inch in diameter—you have two choices. If you're heading, cut back to a bud that is pointing in the direction you want the new growth to go. Ninety-nine percent of the time, that will be an outward-facing bud. Cut about a quarter inch above the bud, and slant the cut away from the bud; with opposite buds, cut straight across the stem. (Cut closer than a quarter inch and you're likely to damage the bud; cut farther away and you'll leave a stub to decay.) Rather than head all stems to the same length, vary their lengths. That way, your plant won't look as if it's had a crew cut.

If you're removing an entire stem or limb—thinning, rather than heading—cut to an outward-facing branch that has a crotch angle of no less than 45 degrees to the branch you're taking off. Be careful, too, that you don't slice into the connective tissue of the branch that will remain—cut about half an inch above the branch you're cutting to.

Large Cuts Big thinning cuts—those made with a saw—are harder on plants than snips made by shears or even loppers. Big wounds close up more slowly, leaving plants open to infection. Always try to cut back to a branch with a diameter that is at least half as great as that of the limb you're removing. When taking off large limbs, either dead or living, be sure to cut to—but not into—the *branch collar*, the swollen area surrounding the base of a limb. Arborists once recommended flush cuts, sawing as close to a limb or trunk as possible. No more. Botanists have discovered that the branch collar helps the plant to form a chemical barrier against pathogens that may attempt to enter through the open wound. It gives the plant protection while it closes up the cut surface with woundwood.

A poorly executed cut caused a large section of bark to tear off.

Pruning Diseased Plants

Reaching for pruners or a saw may not be the best option when dealing with a tree, shrub, or vine that's showing symptoms of disease. A diseased plant is already stressed. Removing a limb or shoot will stress it even more, so be sure that pruning is the correct solution before you do any cutting. The best response to a disease problem depends on the plant species, the extent of the problem, and other factors specific to the situation and local regulations.

Prune diseased limbs only if the problem is confined to a few branches or an isolated area. A branch affected by fire blight should be removed as soon as you notice the problem and before the disease has had a chance to spread. The same goes for branches with cankers.

If a disease has spread throughout a plant, pruning won't get rid of the problem. Lilacs, for example, are susceptible to powdery mildew in summer, but the disease doesn't harm the plant in the long run; it's largely an aesthetic concern. Prune out all the affected branches and you will be left with a few stubs that might or might not recover from the assault. If you're unsure about the problem or its solution, consult a plant professional before you take action. (See "Organizations and Suppliers," page 111).

Once you've decided that a diseased or infected stem needs to be pruned, be sure to remove the problem completely—and don't make it worse. Never prune when plants are wet: Water is a great carrier of disease. Always cut to healthy wood—its pith is white or tan—and always cut well beyond the problem, at least six inches if possible. Be sure to remove and destroy the affected cuttings, and sterilize your pruning tools between cuts by soaking them for one to two minutes in a 10 percent bleach solution (one part bleach, nine parts water) or in isopropyl alcohol.

Just above the branch, on the wood you're cutting *to*, you should be able to see the *branch bark ridge*, a dark bark line that runs approximately parallel to the branch you're removing. You don't want to cut into the branch bark ridge either. Depending on the tree species, the branch collar and the branch bark ridge may be more or less obvious. If you have trouble finding them, look for older pruning cuts on the same tree or another tree of the same species. Cuts that have closed up properly will give you an indication of what the branch attachment looks like and will help you find the right area and the right angle for your pruning cut. (See also "Pruning Entire Branches," page 46.)

To thin a large lateral branch—one more than two inches in diameter—cut as close to the remaining limb or trunk as you can without cutting into the branch bark ridge or the branch collar. The cut should angle away from the wood you're cutting to. It often helps to have another pair of hands to support the branch you're removing so that when it falls, it doesn't damage or strip the bark of the limb or trunk to which it's attached. (If the branch isn't too heavy, use your free hand to provide support and slow the fall.)

The Three-Cut Technique

When removing large limbs it will be necessary to use a three-cut technique to avoid damage. If you'd rather be safe than sorry, use this technique every time you work with a saw rather than hand pruners.

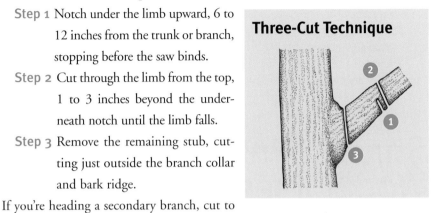

Three-Cut Technique

Step 1 Notch under the limb upward, 6 to 12 inches from the trunk or branch, stopping before the saw binds.

Step 2 Cut through the limb from the top, 1 to 3 inches beyond the underneath notch until the limb falls.

Step 3 Remove the remaining stub, cutting just outside the branch collar and bark ridge.

If you're heading a secondary branch, cut to a limb that is at least one third the diameter of the one you're taking off. Follow a three-cut technique for large limbs so that you don't strip bark from the remaining branch. First, make a V-shaped notch on the side of the branch away from and about eight inches above the node you're cutting to. Second, from the opposite side and just above the notch, make a second cut through the limb. Third, remove the stub. Make your cut as close as possible to the branch collar, but don't cut into the collar or the branch bark ridge. The size and angle of the collar vary greatly from one tree species to the next and vary somewhat between trees of the same species, which means the ideal angle for the cut will be different each time. Don't rush this step: The quality of your final cut determines whether or not the wound will close up properly.

Should Tree Wounds Be Dressed?

As a general rule, don't dress. Tree wound dressings, a.k.a. pruning paints, once were standard treatment for cuts larger than an inch or two. The theory was that they prevented disease and insect damage to (and through) the wound. More recently, researchers have established that bituminous paints and other wound dressings not only don't prevent damage, they may do damage by slowing the formation of wound-wood. (In a very few regions, wound dressings are recommended for particular species as protection against specific diseases; for example, against the spread of oak wilt in some parts of Texas. If you're pruning an old and valuable tree, check with local specialists.)

Shrubs: Pruning the Workhorses of the Garden

Shrubs are garden treasures—and garden workhorses, a major component of what the experts call the "bones" of any landscape plan. They bear colorful leaves, flowers, and fruits; they create backdrops and barriers; they range from tall to ground-hugging, compact to meandering. Many of the most familiar shrubs are deciduous, broadleaf plants that lose their foliage in autumn and then leaf out again in spring.

Unless you're tending a hedge, only a few shrubs demand regular, frequent pruning.

Broadleaf evergreens, in contrast, are shrubs that stay green all year. Some deciduous species—orange ball tree (*Buddleja globosa*), yellow grove bamboo (*Phyllostachys aureosulcata*), and sweet bay (*Magnolia virginiana*) are examples—diverge by location: deciduous in cold climates, evergreen where it stays warm in winter.

A good estimate is that more than half of all shrub pruning is necessary solely because we gardeners choose a big shrub for a little site. It's not only true that *Compost Happens,* as the popular bumper sticker declares, but that *Plants Grow.* If the choice is yours, set a new plant in a spot where it has room to expand, and your pruning tools will spend most of their time in the toolshed, where they belong.

Most shrubs end up being pruned because they have outgrown their alloted space. It is better to select a small shrub such as bush cinquefoil, *Potentilla fruticosa*, for a tight space.

Unless you're tending a hedge, only a few species demand regular, frequent pruning. Shrubs do not need an annual haircut, although most need occasional care. Pruning begins when plants are young. A good start means making sure young plants have strong frameworks—no stems that grow inward or cross, no stems that stray or are weak and unproductive. Container-grown shrubs typically don't need to be pruned at the time of planting, but you may want to cut back bare-root plants by one fourth or one third to compensate for roots lost when they were dug. It's a trade-off: If you prune, you reduce the leaf surface and thereby the amount of water the plant loses due to transpiration through the leaves, but you also reduce the plant's capacity to photosynthesize and build energy reserves.

Know your shrub's needs before you cut: *Daphne × burkwoodii* resents pruning.

Ideally, established shrubs will require nothing beyond maintenance pruning: taking out dead, damaged, and diseased growth; removing suckers and weak, wayward, overly dense growth; and thinning out water sprouts. Although you can shape any shrub, most look far better if you allow them to grow naturally. If you want a compact shrub, plant a bush cinquefoil (*Potentilla*) or a small holly (*Ilex*). Don't try to tame the long shoots of *Forsythia* or Virginia sweetspire (*Itea virginica*) into a tidy doorway shrub.

A few shrubs are downright huffy about being cut back, but most accede to even over-ardent pruners. Before you undertake anything drastic, however, know as much as you can about how your shrub grows and how it will react. Daphnes are famous for resenting secateurs. Rhododendrons, like other species that develop by extending their main stems, are unlikely to sprout new growth if you cut back into old wood. The flowers of beautybush (*Kolkwitzia amabilis*)—American botanist and plant collector E.H. Wilson called it the best flowering shrub ever brought from China—are produced on the same small twigs year after year. Pinch back these shoots and you'll see few of the glorious yellow-throated pink flowers. If "When in doubt, don't" is the golden rule of pruning, "When in doubt about how hard, prune lightly" is the silver rule.

The Right Time to Prune

Shrubs grown for their foliage such as five-leaf aralia (*Eleutherococcus sieboldianus*) and English boxwood (*Buxus sempervirens*) can be pruned at any time. (See also "The Why and When of Pruning," page 6.) Pruning in late summer and fall can produce new growth that won't survive a cold winter, so most experts recommend early spring and summer, especially for major pruning.

With flowering species, pruning times are more important. Bloom season and habit dictate the schedule. Species like winterberry (*Ilex verticillata*), lilacs (*Syringa*), and mock orange (*Philadelphus coronarius*), which bloom in spring or early summer directly on old wood or on new side shoots (called *laterals* or *spurs*) that grow from old wood, should be pruned immediately after they blossom. The exceptions are flowering shrubs that produce fruits or seeds that are worth preserving for their ornamental value or as food for wildlife; these should be pruned lightly before spring growth begins.

Prune rose-of-Sharon (*Hibiscus syriacus*), summersweet (*Clethra alnifolia*), common gardenia (*Gardenia augusta*), and other species that flower in summer and fall on new wood—growth produced in the current season—in late winter or early spring, before they break dormancy.

Making the Cut

There are two basic techniques for shaping and pruning woody plants: thinning and heading. (See "The Kindest Cuts," page 18, for more information.) Many pruning jobs require some of each, as well as some pinching, which is removing the growing end of a shoot. The only tools needed for pinching are your thumbnail and forefinger, but thinning and heading require pruning shears or a pruning saw, not hedge clippers. (For more on tools, see "Outfitting the Pruner," page 100.) Shearing, which is cutting back to keep a plant an exact shape, does require hedge clippers. (Hedges are covered in "Special Cases," page 88.)

Thinning out—removing entire shoots or cutting back to a main trunk—reduces size and stimulates little or no new growth near the cut. Thinning creates a more open form, allows for better air circulation, and permits more light to reach the plant's interior. Thinning also preserves a shrub's natural shape better than heading does.

In contrast, heading—cutting back part of a stem—produces dense growth near the cut on the outside of the plant. When shrubs are regularly headed, the vigorous new growth at the end of the stem tends to shade out the interior foliage and to create top-heavy plants that are awkward looking, even bare legged. If a shrub must be headed to keep it in bounds, cut shoots back to different lengths rather than to one length. Don't forget to cut just above a healthy bud that is facing in the direction you want the new growth to go.

Most authorities agree that deciduous shrubs profit by—but do not require—removing spent flowers before they set seed in order to preserve energy reserves for next year's leaf and flower production. It's the shrub equivalent of *deadheading,* a common practice of flower gardeners, who pick spent blooms in order to promote more flowers and a longer bloom season. Just remember that if you want the fruit or the seedheads, don't remove the flowers.

You can try to renew an old overgrown shrub through severe pruning, but you risk killing the plant.

A Shrub-by-Shrub Guide to Pruning

Keeping in mind that many shrubs don't have to be pruned every year, begin with the basics: Remove dead, damaged, and diseased wood; stems that cross, rub, or head the wrong direction; stems that are weak or unproductive; and unwanted suckers and spent flowers. After those cuts, the general goal when pruning deciduous shrubs is to keep them healthy, vigorous, and productive, and to help them follow their natural shapes.

Abelia × *grandiflora*, glossy abelia, bush arbutus. Flowers on new wood. Prune in late winter to early spring; cut older stems to ground to encourage new growth. Prune hedge plants spring through summer.

Abutilon species, flowering maples. Flower on new growth. Deadhead; pinch stem ends to encourage new sprouts; thin old growth in early spring.

Aesculus parviflora, bottlebrush buckeye. Flowers on old wood. Remove suckers; cut healthy old plants to the ground for renewal.

Amelanchier species, serviceberries, shadblows, juneberries. Flower on old wood. Need little pruning; remove suckers. To preserve fruit crop, prune lightly in early spring.

Arbutus unedo, strawberry tree. Flowers in fall on new wood; ornamental fruits ripen a year following flowering. Prune in early spring as needed; remove suckers promptly.

Aronia arbutifolia, red chokeberry. Flowers in spring on old wood. Prune as needed after flowering; severe pruning will reduce the crop of bright red fruits. Pinch back shoots to encourage bushiness.

Big-leaf hydrangea, *Hydrangea macrophylla,* flowers from buds produced the previous year. Leave flowerheads on plants after blooming and deadhead in spring.

Left and right: Peegee hydrangea, *Hydrangea paniculata*, flowers on new wood. Prune in late winter, cutting stems back to two or three sets of buds, and remove any dead or weak stems.

Artemisia species, southernwoods, wormwoods. Flower on new wood; prune hard in late winter to early spring to keep plants from becoming straggly.

Buddleja alternifolia, fountain butterfly bush. Blossoms on old wood; prune shoots back to old wood after flowering; selectively remove old stems to promote new growth.

Buxus sempervirens, English boxwood, box. Prune as needed, spring through summer; avoid fall pruning, which promotes new growth susceptible to winterkill. Cut back overgrown healthy plants to one foot in spring.

Callicarpa species, beautyberries. Bloom on current season's growth, but don't prune after flowering or you'll lose the ornamental fruits. Annually cut a portion of the oldest stems to six inches in late winter to early spring to promote new growth and a good berry crop.

Calluna vulgaris, Scotch heather. Flowers on new growth. Prune each year in early spring, heading stems back to last year's wood to promote compact growth.

Calycanthus floridus, Carolina allspice, sweetshrub. Flowers on new wood; needs little pruning. Remove oldest shoots as needed in early spring.

Camellia japonica, Japanese camellia. Blooms on old and new wood. Usually needs little pruning. Prune after flowering to thin out old growth and remove over-long stems.

Chaenomeles species, flowering quinces, Japanese quinces. Bloom on old wood. Prune after flowering, cutting oldest stems to the ground. Cut entire plant to six inches to renew.

Chimonanthus praecox, fragrant wintersweet. Blooms on old wood; remove old stems after flowering.

Clethra alnifolia, summersweet, sweet pepperbush. Flowers on new wood; little pruning needed. Remove suckers to control spread; to thin or renew, cut unproductive or weak wood to the ground in late winter.

Cornus stolonifera, red-twig, red osier, dogwood. Cut plants to ground in late winter to produce new growth and the most intense stem color; to control spread, cut oldest stems to ground. Hard pruning also helps control twig blight. Treat *Cornus alba,* Tartarian dogwood, similarly. Root-prune to control spread.

Corylopsis species, winter hazels. Flower on old wood. Give plants plenty of room; prune as little as possible (after flowering) to retain natural habit.

Cotinus coggygria, smokebush, smoke tree. Little pruning needed. Flowers grow on new wood. (The real show, the colorful flower stems, come after the flowers drop.) For foliage alone, head stems back in early spring to second-lowest set of buds. To keep plants small, cut to the ground in late winter to early spring.

Daphne × burkwoodii, Burkwood daphne. Flowers on old wood. Plants are easily stressed, so prune with care after flowering only if necessary.

Deutzia species, deutzias. Bloom on old wood. In early spring remove any winter-damaged stem tips; prune as needed after flowering.

Eleutherococcus sieboldianus, five-leaf aralia. Prune in late winter to early spring by removing entire stems to control growth.

Erica species, heaths, heathers. Winter and spring bloomers should be pruned after flowering ends to ensure vigorous growth; prune summer and fall-flowering heaths in early spring. Cut annually to within an inch of the previous year's growth. Do not cut back into old wood, which will not produce new shoots.

Forsythia species, forsythias, golden bells. Bloom on old wood. Allow to follow natural form. To promote new growth and flowering, cut a quarter of canes to the ground after flowering each year, or thin out oldest shoots.

Fothergilla species, fothergillas, witch alders. Bloom on old wood; prune as needed after flowering.

Gardenia augusta, common gardenia. Flowers on new wood. Prune in late winter to early spring before new growth begins.

Hamamelis species, witch hazels. Most species bloom on old wood in winter and early spring. Need little pruning beyond removing dead wood; cuts are often slow to close up. Remove suckers; prune as needed after flowering. Remove individual stems to control height. *Hamamelis virginiana,* common witch hazel, flowers in autumn.

Shrub Maintenance Pruning

Do maintenance pruning when the plant is dormant: Take out dead, damaged, weak, wayward, and overly dense growth, shown in gray.

Hibiscus syriacus, shrub althea, rose-of-Sharon. Flowers on current season's wood. Prune if necessary in late winter to early spring while dormant. Cut plants to six inches to renew. Prune *Hibiscus rosa-sinensis,* Chinese hibiscus, in spring.

Hydrangea species, hydrangeas. Better too little pruning than too much with big-leaf hydrangea (*Hydrangea macrophylla*), which flowers from buds produced the previous year. Leave flower heads on plants after blooming; in early spring, deadhead by cutting back to just above the first pair of healthy buds, and prune one fourth of oldest stems to the ground to reduce crowding. To renew an old plant, prune severely in midsummer. *Hydrangea paniculata,* the peegee hydrangea, and *H. arborescens,* hills-of-snow, flower on new wood. Prune in late winter, cutting stems back to two or three sets of buds; remove any dead or weak stems. Prune oak-leaf hydrangea (*H. quercifolia*), which blooms on old wood, after flowering by removing dead or weak stems; cut one fourth of older stems to the ground every two to three years to reduce crowding.

Ilex species, hollies. Leaves and berries, not flowers, are the goal with evergreen hollies, such as *Ilex cornuta, I. opaca,* and *I.* × *meserveae.* Most need little pruning. Clip hedge plants in spring or summer (and trim again in mid-December). Prune deciduous winterberry (*I. verticillata*) in early spring in order to spare its ornamental drupes.

Itea virginica, Virginia sweetspire, Virginia willow. Blossoms on old wood; prune after flowering ends. Needs little pruning. Root-prune to control spread.

Kalmia latifolia, mountain laurel. Flowers on old wood; prune and deadhead after

Prune oleander, *Nerium oleander,* in early spring to control size. Renew by removing the oldest canes. Oleander leaves and stems are toxic, even when burned. Dispose of them carefully.

blossoms fade. Little to no pruning needed. Renewal pruning—cutting the shrub to six inches—is very precarious, and the plant is slow to grow back.

Kerria japonica, kerria, Japanese rose. Blooms on old wood. Systematically remove oldest woody stems after flowering to promote vigor.

Kolkwitzia amabilis, beautybush. Flowers on old wood; little pruning needed. Remove weak stems growing from the main branches after flowering; cut oldest stems to the ground to renew.

Lagerstroemia indica, crape myrtle. Flowers on new wood. Never top plants. Prune lightly in late winter to early spring for larger flowers; to encourage a second bloom, remove spent flowers. Prune seed heads to just above a lateral bud.

Lindera benzoin, spicebush. Flowers on old wood. To preserve ornamental fruits, prune lightly in late winter or early spring. Requires little pruning. Cut old, overgrown plants to the ground to renew.

Invasive Shrubs

The following shrubs often grown in gardens can be invasive in natural areas. Check with botanical gardens or preserve managers in your area before planting them.

Berberis species, barberries
Buddleja davidii, butterfly bush
Cotoneaster species, cotoneasters
Cytisus scoparius, Scotch broom
Elaeagnus umbellata, autumn olive
Elaeagnus angustifolia, Russian olive
Euonymus alatus, burning bush
Ilex aquifolium, English holly
Ligustrum species, privets
Lonicera species, bush honeysuckles
Nandina domestica, heavenly bamboo
Scaevola sericea (*S. taccada*), beach naupaka
Spiraea japonica, Japanese spirea
Tamarix species, tamarisks
Viburnum opulus var. *opulus,* guelder rose

Mahonia species, Oregon grapes, grape hollies. Flower on old wood; little pruning needed. Cut old, woody shoots to the ground to renew.

Nerium oleander, oleander, rosebay. Prune in early spring to control size. Renew by removing oldest canes. (Oleander leaves and stems are toxic, even when burned; dispose of them carefully.)

Philadelphus species, mock oranges. Bloom on old wood; prune annually after flowering by cutting back flowering stems to a strong bud. Cut oldest stems to the ground to renew.

Photinia × fraseri, redtip, Fraser's potenia. Blooms on old wood; prune after flowering. Needs little pruning, but heading stems annually promotes the crop of new, bright red leaves.

Pieris species, pierises. Pierises, including lily-of-the-valley bush (*Pieris japonica*), mountain pieris (*P. floribunda*), and the hybrid 'Brouwer's Beauty', flower in spring on old wood; prune after flowering. Need little pruning.

Potentilla fruticosa, bush cinquefoil. Blooms on new wood; prune in late winter to early spring by cutting a third of the oldest stems to the ground.

Prunus species, flowering cherries, sand-plums, flowering almonds. Flower on old wood. Most species need little pruning. Cut back the flowering shoots of dwarf flowering almond (*Prunus tenella*) as soon as the blooms fade. Cherry-laurel (*P. laurocerasus*) tolerates hard pruning.

Pyracantha species, pyracanthas, firethorns. Flower on last season's growth. To preserve berries, prune lightly in late winter to early spring; otherwise, prune after flowering to encourage branching by heading back new growth beyond the fruit clusters.

Rhododendron species, rhododendrons, azaleas. Both rhododendrons and azaleas bloom on old wood; prune immediately after flowering. Cut dying stems back to healthy green wood; pinch new stems to stimulate branching. Old woody stems are unlikely to resprout. Do not remove more than a quarter of a plant's stems when renewing. Rhododendrons and azaleas are shallow-rooted.

Rhus aromatica, fragrant sumac. Requires little pruning; cut errant or overly tall stems to the ground in early spring.

Rosa species, roses. See page 76.

Salix species, pussy willows. Shrub willows, such as *Salix discolor, S. elaeagnos,* and *S. caprea,* flower on old wood; prune after flowering. For long stems and many catkins, cut all (or a portion of) stems to six inches every year.

Skimmia japonica, Japanese skimmia. Little pruning required. Blooms on old wood. Prune after flowering; or, to preserve fruits, prune lightly in early spring.

Sorbaria species, false spireas. Flower on new wood. Prune in late winter to early spring while still dormant.

Spiraea species, spireas. Bridalwreath (*Spiraea prunifolia*), garland spirea (*S. × arguta*), and other early-flowering species bloom on last year's growth; prune after flowering. Billard (*S. × billardii*), Bumald (*S. × bumalda*), and other summer-flowering spireas bloom on new wood; prune in late winter to early spring. Most need little pruning; thin oldest stems to maintain vigor and reduce crowding.

Symphoricarpos species, coralberries, snowberries, waxberries. Flower on new wood; prune as needed in late winter to early spring by cutting back entire shoots. Remove suckers to control spread.

Syringa species, lilacs. Lilacs flower on wood produced the previous season; prune after flowering ends by removing spent flower heads and cutting weak, crowded, and unproductive wood to the ground. Remove any suckers that sprout from the root-

From Shrub to Tree

The difference between shrubs and trees is largely a matter of form: Shrubs typically have multiple stems, whereas trees usually have only one. Many shrubs can be converted to small trees by early and careful pruning.

In early spring
- Form the trunk by selecting a single stem (or two or three) and cutting back all other stems to the ground.
- Limb up—remove any lateral shoots—the bottom third of the remaining stems.

The next year
- Limb up to the height you want.
- Prune and shape the crown as needed.
- Remove any lateral shoots that sprout from the "trunk."
- Remove any suckers.
- Once the desired form is established, prune as you would a deciduous tree.

Willing candidates for this transformation are often labeled "shrub or small tree" in garden books and on nursery tags. Japanese and tartarian maples (*Acer palmatum, A. tataricum*), pagoda dogwood (*Cornus alternifolia*), hollies (*Ilex*), serviceberries (*Amelanchier*), rose-of-Sharon (*Hibiscus syriacus*), European filbert (*Corylus avellana*), smokebush (*Cotinus coggygria*), chaste tree (*Vitex agnus-castus*), fragrant winter hazel (*Corylopsis glabrescens*), witch hazels (*Hamamelis*), crape myrtle (*Lagerstroemia indica*), camellia (*Camellia japonica*), and small magnolia species are some of the usual suspects.

stock of lilacs grafted on common lilac or privet. To renew an old, overgrown lilac, either cut the entire plant back to eight inches in late winter, or—a safer option—cut a third of the stems back to eight inches of the ground each year for three years. Thin the new shoots, heading back those you keep to encourage branching.

Viburnum **species, viburnums.** Deciduous viburnums, including American cranberry bush (*Viburnm trilobum*), Korean spice viburnum (*V. carlesii*), Japanese snowball (*V. plicatum* f. *plicatum*), doublefile viburnum (*V. plicatum* f. *tomentosum*), nannyberry (*V. lentago*), and black haw (*V. prunifolium*), flower on old wood; prune after flowering if necessary. To preserve ornamental fruits, prune lightly in early spring by removing old and weak stems. Do not head back. To renew and reduce crowding, cut a portion of oldest stems to the ground each year. Prune less hardy evergreen viburnums in late winter.

Weigela florida, **weigela.** Flowers on old wood; prune after flowering. Cut a portion of the oldest stems to the ground each year; to encourage blooming, head back vigorous flowering stems by half.

Deciduous Trees: Pruning the Garden's Monuments

"The best monuments that man can erect to his own memory." That's what the second Earl of Orrery, an Irish statesman and writer, said of trees in 1749. Parents may challenge that declaration, but whether zoological or botanical, monuments need care. Trees need less attention than children, but they do need attention, especially pruning attention, and especially when they're young.

Any pruning cut on a deciduous tree—a tree that drops its leaves in autumn, enters a period of dormancy, and then sprouts new leaves in spring—has the power to change its size, form, and health. The more severe the pruning, the more risk it carries. The 16th-century English poet Robert Southwell insisted that "the lopped tree in time may grow again." Put an accent on that *may*. It may not grow again.

So be sure you are clear about what you want to accomplish and know what you're doing before you start lopping. Trees, like most plants, are amazingly tolerant, but even little pruning mistakes

You'll reduce the need for pruning tenfold if you choose the right plant from the get-go.

Opposite: Any pruning cut on a mature deciduous tree such as sugar maple, *Acer saccharum*, has the power to change its size, form, and health.

can have big consequences, especially if they are repeated year after year. Moreover, pruning won't compensate for problems caused by poor soil, poor drainage, drought, diseases and insects, or a poor site. In fact, pruning an already stressed tree makes things worse.

You'll reduce the need for pruning tenfold if you choose the right plant from the get-go. It should be hardy in your location; a tree too tender for your climate will suffer winterkill and need regular trimming. And it needs to be planted where it will have the soil and light conditions it requires as well as enough room to mature. The worst error, one that will haunt you forever, is to plant a big tree in a little space.

Every homeowner makes mistakes when placing trees in the landscape, and you've probably inherited at least one of these errors. Even the right tree in the right climate in the right place requires some pruning, occasional cutting, and sawing to eliminate hazards, to train and shape, to encourage flowering and fruiting, to control growth, and to maintain good health. The aim in pruning trees is to help them to be healthy, strong, beautiful, and enduring.

Tree Basics

Anyone planning to prune a tree should know a bit about roots, trunks, branches, and leaves, the main parts that make up a tree. *Roots* hold the tree in the ground and absorb water and nutrients. *Trunks,* or main stems—some trees, such as star magnolia (*Magnolia stellata*) often have multiple trunks—support branches and provide a conduit for water

and nutrients to travel from the roots to the leaves and, after photosynthesis, for the manufactured food to move from the leaves back to the roots. *Branches*, extensions of the trunk, are also conduits and support the leaves and flowers. *Leaves* shade the trunk and branches and make the food that a tree needs to grow. And, when talking about deciduous trees, you could add *flowers*, which produce the seeds that ensure a tree's immortality.

Tree trunks and branches differ in size, not structure. They contain spongy core tissue, or pith, surrounded in many

A weak branch union is vulnerable to breaking.

Knowing how a tree wants to grow is an important part of knowing how to prune it. Above is a mature white oak, *Quercus alba,* an example of a tree with a large, spreading canopy.

cases by heartwood, surrounded by water-conducting sapwood, surrounded by cambium, surrounded by bark, inner and outer. If you *girdle* a tree—remove the bark all the way around a trunk or branch, exposing or damaging the cambium—the result is usually fatal. (Girdle a branch, and everything above the cut will die.) Deer and rodents are notorious bark girdlers, but weed trimmers, lawn mowers, and cars also take a toll on trees. Even cuts on only a portion of a branch or trunk are enough to stunt growth.

Acorns to Oaks

Remember that trick question on high school science tests: "If a tree branch is ten feet from the ground and the tree grows one foot each year, how far from the ground will the branch be in ten years?" No, not 20 feet. Ten feet. Branches on a tree trunk stay at the same height because growth occurs in tissues located in the cambium and the buds (and in the root tips). Trunks and branches increase in girth thanks to the cell division in the cambium and grow in length from cell division in the buds. T&T: Trees grow from their tips and tops.

Buds are programmed to produce stems, leaves, and flowers, either in one fell swoop in spring or throughout the growing season. *Terminal,* or *apical, buds* are those at the tips of branches. A tree's height and spread come from terminal buds. *Lateral buds* are buds located at nodes along branches. Those that occur along the trunk form branches; lateral buds on branches produce secondary branches, leaves, and flowers.

Tree shape is determined largely by the phenomenon called *apical dominance,* the influence of the terminal bud over the lateral buds. (For more on apical dominance, see "The Why and When of Pruning," page 6.) In trees like sweet gum (*Liquidambar styraciflua*) and shagbark hickory (*Carya ovata*), which have fairly strong apical dominance, the trunk grows more than the branches, and branches attached to the trunk grow more than secondary branches. The result is a tree with a strong *central leader,* one main stem, and a pyramidal form. It is a growth habit called *excurrent* and is most pronounced in conifers.

Most mature deciduous trees are *decurrent*, not excurrent, and lack the strong apical dominance that conifers display. Their main stem and primary and secondary branches grow pretty much at the same rate, and they take shapes other than pyramidal, everything from round and columnar to vase and weeping. They may have more than one main stem—called *modified leaders*—and often have large, spreading canopies as red oak (*Quercus rubra*) and Washington hawthorn (*Crataegus phaenopyrum*) do.

A third growth habit, more rare, is *fastigiate.* Fastigiate trees have long branches that grow nearly straight up to create living columns. You may even find the words "fastigiate" or "column" in their botanical names: the columnar European beech (*Fagus sylvatica* 'Fastigiata') and the columnar red maple (*Acer rubrum* 'Columnare') are examples. Knowing how your tree wants to grow is an important part of knowing how to prune it.

For the biggest, tallest tree on the block, do as little pruning as possible. For the strongest, healthiest tree, one that will outlive everyone on the block, some pruning is necessary. Unless you have an important reason to do otherwise—such as keeping limbs out of power lines or removing limbs damaged in a storm—take out as few of a tree's live branches at one time as possible. Removing foliage reduces a tree's capacity to manufacture the sugars that propel and sustain its growth. Remove a substantial number of branches and leaves at one time and you threaten a tree's ability to survive. If you must eliminate many limbs, spread the task out over several seasons.

Pruning Effects

Late winter or early spring, just before dormancy ends, is the best time to prune most trees in most regions, although some maples (*Acer*), lindens (*Tilia*), and willows (*Salix*),

While they were still young, the goldenrain tree, *Koelreuteria paniculata,* on the left, and the pyramidal English oak, *Quercus robur,* on the right, were pruned to make them strong and follow their natural shapes. Now that they have grown into mature trees, they require very little or no corrective pruning.

Natural Shapes

Unless you have a very compelling reason to do otherwise, allow trees to follow their natural predilections, to adhere to their inborn forms. European beech (*Fagus sylvatica*), pin oak (*Quercus palustris*), and sweet gum (*Liquidambar styraciflua*) have a pyramidal, or conical, shape; white oak *(Quercus alba)*, red maple (*Acer rubrum*), and horsechestnut (*Aesculus hippocastanum*) develop a rounded form as they mature; white willow (*Salix alba*) and European white birch (*Betula pendula*) have pendulous stems; while the branches of the pagoda dogwood (*Cornus alternifolia*) grow horizontally. Between Mother Nature and the breeders, trees know where they're going. You'll never convert a Lombardy popular (*Populus nigra* var. *italica*) into a spreading tree that Longfellow's village smithy would recognize. Don't try.

species that lose large amounts of sap when they are cut in late winter or early spring, can also be pruned in summer when they shed less sap. Before leaves open is the time to see and evaluate a tree's structure, and the time when wounds close most quickly. Avoid heavy pruning in fall, which removes the food that's stored in the leaves and branches before the tree can translocate it to the trunk and roots. Fall pruning also stimulates new growth that is susceptible to winterkill. Postpone pruning species that are susceptible to diseases contracted through pruning wounds until pathogens are inactive. For example, trees that are susceptible to fire blight, a bacterial disease that is easily spread in spring and summer by pruning, should always be pruned during the dormant season, late winter to early spring. Be sure to clean your tools before

Pruning Entire Branches

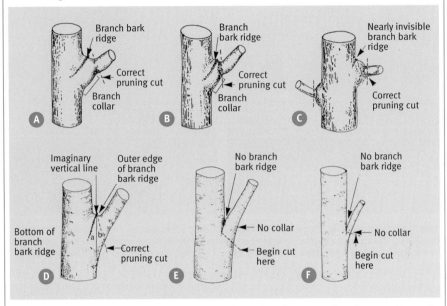

To remove a limb, cut it off just outside the branch collar. Branch collars and branch bark ridges vary according to tree species and age. On some trees, the branch collar is obvious (A and B); the dashed line indicates the correct pruning cut. Trunks form large collars around the base of low, horizontal branches on older trees (C), typically indicating a weak or dying limb on some species; cut just outside the collar. When the bottom of the branch collar is hard to see (D), estimate angle *a* by drawing an imaginary vertical line parallel with the trunk. Beginning on top of the branch at the outer edge of the branch bark ridge, make a pruning cut so angle *b* is the same as angle *a*; the cut often ends even with the bottom of the branch bark ridge. Cut a branch forming a weak, V-shaped union with no collar or branch bark ridge (E and F) along the dashed line. The cut should end where the branch and trunk tissue meet; this may be several inches (young trees) or feet (older trees) down into the branch union. The cut may have to be finished with a chisel to prevent injury of trunk tissue.

moving from one tree to another. (Soak them in a 10 percent bleach solution for one to two minutes.) Among the usual fire blight victims are apples and crabapples (*Malus*), and hawthorns (*Crataegus*). Local authorities will know if any trees may need special timing vis-à-vis pruning in your area. (See "The Why and When of Pruning," page 6, for more on the timing of pruning.)

Whatever the time of year, when you prune trees

- Use clean or sterile, sharp tools.
- Always cut to a bud, a lateral branch, or the main trunk.

- Don't leave stubs, which are entry points for insects and diseases.
- Use a three-step cut (see page 27) for large limbs, those more than two inches in diameter.
- Don't dress the wound.

Each time you cut, the tree releases hormones that alert buds just below the cut to sprout. That phenomenon gives you considerable control over the direction the tree will or won't grow, so you'll want to cut to an outward-growing bud almost every time. Most tree pruning should be *thinning*—removing an entire limb—rather than *heading back*, which is cutting off part of a limb. Heading cuts encourage *epicormic* sprouts, or *water* sprouts, ugly, weakly attached vertical shoots, and excessive tip growth. Thinning doesn't promote this type of vigorous growth and preserves the tree's natural shape. (For more on the effects of pruning, see "The Why and When of Pruning," page 6, and "The Kindest Cuts," page 18.)

It's usually wise to start at the top of any woody plant and prune down. Each

Before you cut, find the branch collar and the branch bark ridge. Cut just at the branch collar but not into it. Cutting flush with the trunk as shown above will expose the tree to pathogens.

cut should be as close to the remaining branch as possible—but *never* cut flush, into the *branch collar*, the swollen ring of tissue around the base of a branch, or the *branch bark ridge*, the line of dark, wrinkled bark that runs between the branch you're removing and the one that remains. They work together to close off the wound and protect the tree from pathogens. (If *callus tissue*, or *woundwood*, forms around the wound, it's sealing well, and your cut was just right.)

Flush cuts invite pathogens to enter and spread throughout the tree, and they are slow to close, if they close at all. What's more, in many tree species they cause dozens of water sprouts to emerge from latent buds around the wound, a sure sign of stress.

The aim in pruning trees is to help them be healthy, strong, beautiful, and enduring, and the right timing is key to ensure these goals. If sourwood, *Oxydendrum arboreum,* needs pruning at all, it should be done in late spring to preserve the ornamental fruits that form in fall.

Cleaning out *mare's nests* or *lion's tails,* dense clusters of water sprouts, is a chore for any-one who inherits badly pruned trees, especially flowering crabapples and fruit trees. The best approach is usually to thin out most of the sprouts and leave a few behind to discourage the tree from sending up more.

Young and Old

As a group, most trees do fine with minimal pruning after they are established. Age is peremptory when it comes to pruning trees: Young trees may need a strong hand, while old-timers benefit from benign neglect. Some pruning jobs apply to all trees of all ages, at any time of year:

- Remove limbs that pose hazards to people or property.
- Remove damaged and dead wood.

- Remove crowded or crossing branches and branches with unnaturally narrow branch unions.
- Remove suckers and thin out water sprouts.
- Remove small *girdling roots,* roots that encircle the trunk.

Whatever its age, a tree recovers better and quicker from a series of small pruning cuts than it does from one big cut. And whatever its age, always have the tree's natural form uppermost in your mind. If you're not sure if a branch union is "unnaturally narrow" or just as nature intended it to be, take a closer look at some other trees of the same species and compare.

Caring for Very Young Trees

New trees need every leaf and stem to produce food for root development, so prune as little as possible after planting. Remove any damaged or dead branches on a container-grown or balled-and-burlapped tree, then put away your pruning shears. If yours is a bare-root or freshly dug tree, first cut off any damaged or dead roots. You may want to thin a few stems to compensate for lost or damaged roots, but don't head back the central leader. You can remove a competing leader, especially if the two join in a narrow, weak branch union.

Pruning a young tree for strength and form comes after it's established, two or three years post-planting. Informed pruning then and during the next few years will mean little or no corrective work when the tree is mature. Be aware of its natural shape and prune to preserve that form. The additional objectives are to create a strong trunk and strong, well-placed, and well-spaced scaffold branches, the main lateral limbs that come off the trunk.

Unless you've planted a small ornamental species like a Japanese maple (*Acer palmatum*) that is enhanced by multiple trunks, encouraging the central leader is the first job. Its lower section will be the trunk of the tree. If there is competition, choose one shoot for the central leader and remove any rivals. (Even trees whose mature crowns will be rounded, such as pecan [*Carya illinoinensis*], need to start off with one strong central leader.) Lateral branches make food to produce a thick, sturdy trunk, so don't rush to remove low ones, known as *temporary branches,* even if you want the first lateral limb ten feet up. The unbranched trunk of a young tree should not be more than a third of the tree's height. Low limbs can be pruned off later.

The strength of lateral branches depends on their relative size, their placement, and the angle at which they grow from the trunk. Although there is variation depending on the tree species, there are some general guidelines most experts follow.

- Don't let lateral branches outpace the leader—in girth or length.
- Space lateral branches evenly, establishing both radial and vertical balance. Good spacing not only weight-balances the tree, it prevents one limb from over-shadowing another.

There should be branches growing out from all sides of the trunk; don't let two branches grow directly above each other on the same side of the tree.

Use the 3 percent rule for vertical spacing: The distance between scaffold limbs should be about 3 percent of the tree's mature height. For example, the lateral limbs on the trunk of a river birch (*Betula nigra*) with an expected height of 50 feet should be about 18 inches apart.

- For greatest strength, lateral branches should attach to the trunk at an angle between 45 and 60 degrees. Branches with unnaturally narrow angles often develop compressed and dead, or *included,* bark in the branch union that stops normal growth and weakens the joint. The only exceptions are trees with naturally narrow branch unions, such as elms (*Ulmus*), *Zelkova,* and some oaks (*Quercus*).
- Never cut all the limbs on a tree back to the same length. If you must shorten a lateral branch, cut back to a branch or bud.
- If you must limit height, start when the tree is still young by cutting the central leader back to a small lateral branch.

Caring for Mature Trees

If you've done your work well, your mature tree will have a robust trunk and leader, and well-spaced and properly angled lateral branches. Maintenance and prevention are uppermost now, pruning to keep the tree healthy and attractive, and the people and things near it safe. Many mature trees can go five or ten years without pruning, but occasionally even they need attention beyond maintenance trimming.

Three activities are most common: pruning to clean the canopy, pruning to reduce, or thin, the canopy, and pruning to lift the canopy. (For more on pruning techniques, see "The Kindest Cuts," page 18.) *Cleaning the canopy* involves thinning water sprouts and cutting out dead and damaged wood; errant, weak, and crowded branches; and limbs with weak crotches. *Thinning the canopy* means decreasing its size and weight by removing entire limbs. When you can, thin smaller branches rather than large ones.

Sometimes cutting the central leader back to a large lateral branch, or *drop crotch-ing,* becomes necessary. Make the cut on an angle parallel to the branch bark ridge of the limb you're cutting to. The limb you cut to should have a good union angle, 45 to 60 degrees. Never drop crotch to a horizontal limb—the pros call it a *bench cut*—which will produce more water sprouts than you can count.

Raising the canopy, removing lower branches, is the easiest activity, not out of reach for home pruners. For the most part, though, pruning sizable trees is something better left to the professionals.

There also is universal agreement about *topping,* or *stubbing,* a tree, heading back all the limbs of its canopy. Topping reduces size, but all its other effects are negative. It leaves stubs that are open to decay; it encourages crowded epicormic growth that is weakly attached and vulnerable to damage; and worst of all, it produces a tree that is an eyesore. Not fit to be seen. Blood-sucking ugly. If a tree is so large that topping is the only solution, replace the tree. And if a professional recommends topping a tree, replace him or her.

Be aware that not all trees react to severe pruning in the same way. Oaks (*Quercus*), poplars (*Populus*), and lindens (*Tilia*), for instance, are notably forbearing about major-league cutting and sawing; maples (*Acer*), ashes (*Fraxinus*), and sycamores (*Platanus*) less so; and beeches (*Fagus*), birches (*Betula*), and hornbeams (*Carpinus*) less so still. Severe pruning is always chancy for a grown tree.

Flower Fundamentals

Although flowering trees typically need far less pruning than flowering shrubs and vines do, the same rules apply for when to prune. These are designed to keep you from removing flower buds before they open. Prune spring bloomers, such as dogwood (*Cornus florida*) and eastern redbud (*Cercis canadensis*), after their blossoms fade; prune late-summer and fall bloomers like Franklin tree (*Franklinia alatamaha*), golden-rain tree (*Koelreuteria paniculata*), and crape myrtle (*Lagerstroemia indica*), in early spring before buds open. You may want to ignore the rules for deciduous trees that bloom in spring and produce ornamental fruits in summer and fall; to preserve the handsome fruits of kousa dogwood (*Cornus kousa*), cockspur hawthorn (*Crataegus crus-galli*), and their like, do most of your pruning in late winter to early spring.

A Tree-by-Tree Guide to Pruning

While most deciduous trees aren't cranky, some need special treatment or timing when pruned. This very selective list includes some of the most popular flowering species as well as a few nonflowering trees that may pose pruning questions. See the box "Pruning Diseased Plants," page 26, for guidelines on pruning diseased trees.

Albizia julibrissin, silk tree, mimosa. Train to multiple trunks; prune in early spring.

Amelanchier × grandiflora, apple serviceberry. Train to single or multiple trunks. Prune to shape after blooming ends; remove unwanted suckers.

Catalpa bignonioides, southern catalpa. Train to a single, strong trunk; watch for weak branch angles.

Cercis canadensis, eastern redbud. Blooms in early spring; prune after flowering ends. Train to single or multiple trunks; needs little or no pruning.

Chionanthus virginicus, white fringe tree, old-man's beard. Prune as needed after flowering ends; to preserve colorful drupes, prune in early spring. Train as single or multistem tree.

Cladrastis lutea, yellowwood. Yellowwood has brittle wood and saps heavily; prune in summer. Watch for weak branch angles.

Cornus species, dogwoods. Tree species need little or no pruning; allow tree dogwoods to follow their natural form. Train to single or multiple trunks. Prune after blossoms fade, or, to preserve colorful fruits, prune in early spring.

Corylus avellana 'Contorta', Harry Lauder's walking stick. Trees grown on grafted rootstock; remove suckers promptly. Prune in early spring.

Cotinus coggygria, smokebush, smoke tree. See page 34.

Crataegus species, hawthorns. Prune in late winter to early spring to preserve ornamental drupes. Do not over-thin. For safety, remove low-hanging limbs of thorned hawthorns.

Franklinia alatamaha, Franklin tree. Prune in late winter to early spring. Train to multiple trunks; needs little pruning.

Halesia tetraptera, Carolina silverbell, snowdrop tree. Prune after flowering ends only if needed. Allow low limbs to develop.

Koelreuteria paniculata, goldenrain tree, varnish tree. Train to either single or multiple trunks.

Lagerstroemia indica, crape myrtle. See page 36.

Magnolia species, magnolias. Little pruning needed; magnolia wood is brittle, and trees are slow to close up large cuts. Train to single or multiple trunks.

Malus species, crabapples. Prune young trees to either a single leader or an open branching head; to retain ornamental fruits, prune in late winter to early spring. Remove suckers, especially those growing from below the union on grafted trees, and thin water sprouts. Use clean tools to avoid spreading diseases.

Oxydendrum arboreum, sourwood, sorrel tree, lily-of-the-valley tree. Needs little pruning; prune in late spring to preserve ornamental fruits.

Prunus species, flowering cherry, flowering plum. Prune young trees to either a single leader or open branching head according to their natural bent; to retain ornamental fruits, prune in late winter to early spring. Limb up Amur choke-cherry (*Prunus maackii*) to reveal its lustrous bark. Remove suckers and thin out water sprouts.

Sophora japonica, Japanese pagoda tree, scholar tree. Prune to a central leader. Wounds sap heavily; prune late summer to early fall, not spring

Sorbus species, mountain ashes. Prune in winter to early spring to preserve the ornamental red-orange fruits. Prune for strong structure; remove unwanted suckers.

Stewartia species, stewartias. Do not prune young trees; remove suckers. Stewartias need little pruning.

Syringa reticulata, Japanese tree lilac. Prune when flowering ends; little pruning is needed. Train to single or multiple trunks.

Vitex agnus-castus, chaste tree. Train to single or multiple trunks.

Ziziphus jujuba, Chinese date, Chinese jujuba. Prune to encourage weeping habit; prune in late winter to preserve ornamental fruits.

Invasive Trees

The following trees commonly found in gardens can be invasive in natural areas. Check with botanical gardens or preserve managers before planting them. For information on other trees that may be invasive in your area check with your regional Pest Plant Council.

Acer ginnala, Amur maple
Acer platanoides, Norway maple
Broussonetia papyrifera, paper mulberry
Melia azedarach, chinaberry tree
Paulownia tomentosa, princess tree
Pyrus calleryana, callery pear
Sapium sebiferum, Chinese tallow tree

Conifers: Pruning Coniferous Trees and Shrubs

Conifers are about as close to prune-free as woody plants get—if they are growing in a spot where they have room to grow. A properly sited conifer needs next to no pruning, but no group of woody plants is more often planted in cramped quarters. Overgrown foundation evergreens—arborvitaes (*Thuja*), firs (*Picea*), yews (*Taxus*), and more—are as common as dandelions in lawns. And who hasn't passed a house with two Colorado spruces not framing but blocking the front door?

Although the category of conifer includes some of the largest woody plants known, the good news for gardeners is that there are pocket editions of almost every conifer species. And there is practically every shape. The Colorado spruce (*Picea pungens*), for example, is available in pyramidal, upright pyramidal, broad pyramidal, narrow pyramidal, columnar, conical, mound, hemispherical, globose, weeping, low-spreading, and prostrate forms, and the lights are still on in the breeders' laboratories.

With enough light, space, water, and nutrients, many firs, pines, and spruces will grow into attractive, symmetrical shapes without any pruning. Above is eastern white pine, *Pinus strobus* 'Verkade's Broom'. Opposite is Norway spruce, *Picea abies*.

Many conifers respond with dieback if you cut into old wood. So be sure to choose the right-size plant. Above is a dwarf cultivar of blue spruce, *Picea pungens*, that fits into a small garden.

These days, there's no excuse for planting a conifer that can't comfortably inhabit its location for a lifetime. Have 20 acres? Go ahead and plant a *Picea pungens*. Midsize yard? *Picea pungens* 'Tiffin'. Pint-size yard? *Picea pungens* 'Glauca Globosa'. They all come up blue spruces. If you are forever fighting to keep a conifer small—or to conform it to a shape that isn't natural—haul down your colors and replace it.

While most of us think of conifers as Christmas trees, trees with needles that stay green year-round, the word *conifer* actually means "to bear cones." That's true of nearly all conifers, although exceptions include junipers (*Juniperus*) and yews (*Taxus*), which produce their seeds in berrylike cones. Nor do all conifers have needle leaves; arborvitaes (*Thuja*) and false cypresses (*Chamaecyparis*) are two genera with scalelike leaves. Not all conifers are evergreen, either: The common larch (*Larix decidua*) and the common bald cypress (*Taxodium distichum*) both lose their leaves in fall, as does the dawn redwood (*Metasequoia glyptostroboides*). And don't forget, hundreds of conifers aren't shaped like Christmas trees.

Follow the Leader

In *Mountain Interval* (1920), Robert Frost describes his woods filled with balsam firs as "like a place/Where houses all are churches and have spires." It must be the most poetic expression of *apical dominance* on record. The majority of conifers are poster children for apical dominance: a strong *central stem,* or *trunk,* that grows more than the lateral branches and produces a tree with a pyramidal or Christmas tree shape. It is a growth habit known as *excurrent.*

Firs (*Abies*), pines (*Pinus*), and spruces are among the most dependably excurrent and produce their *scaffold,* or *main lateral branches* in whorls around the central stem. They want to be symmetrical. Holster your pruning shears and give them their way—and enough light, space, water, and nutrients—and they will grow into near-perfect green cones.

Other conifer trees, including arborvitaes (*Thuja*), cedars (*Cedrus*), cypresses (*Cupressus*), false cypresses (*Chamaecyparis*), hemlocks (*Tsuga*), junipers (*Juniperus*), and yews (*Taxus*), have irregularly spaced lateral branches, more like deciduous trees do. Many of these trees are still strongly excurrent, but this group of conifers is likely to develop more than one main stem, or leader. In time, all conifers tend to flatten out at the top, to lose their conical form. (That's because apical dominance declines as trees grow older.) Conifers with irregularly spaced branches tend to become asymmetric and flatten out sooner that those with whorled limbs. (For more on growth patterns and apical dominance, see "The Why and When of Pruning," page 6.)

Finally, conifers differ in when they grow. Some are *determinate,* such as pines, and do their growing in one *flush* in the spring. Hemlocks are *semideterminate*: They flush in spring, and then once (or several times) again if growing conditions are good. Junipers flush throughout the garden season, a growth habit known as *indeterminate.*

Since all conifers do some growing in spring, just before growth begins is a good time for major pruning. With new growth on the heels of your cuts, wounds seal quickly and any bare, inner branches you expose are soon obscured by new needles. Needles, remember, are leaves; they produce sugars through photosynthesis just as the foliage of maples (*Acer*) and oaks (*Quercus*) does. If you remove large amounts of new needles after the first flush, your tree or shrub will have less food to use and store. That can be critical, especially in a young conifer, which has few reserves. Late-spring pruning will keep conifers small, but it carries a risk.

Conifer Shrubs

Like conifer trees, most conifer shrubs require little or no pruning. The general rules for pruning trees, such as when and how much to cut off, also apply to shrubs, but there are some differences. Many shrubby conifers lack a central leader—don't try to create one. Use thinning cuts to limit their size. Unless you want a formal shape, don't shear shrubs; instead, remove individual branches or cut back to another branch to preserve a natural look. Strongly horizontal conifer shrubs, such as creeping junipers (*Juniperus horizontalis*), tend to become overly dense as they mature. Thinning the canopy will reduce interior dieback and help prevent problems with insects and diseases.

Calculating the Cuts

If the slicing and sawing you have in mind is more a matter of aesthetics, such as thinning a wayward limb, than it is of health, wait until early spring to take out your tools. Maintenance pruning and care, though, should be done whenever they are needed. Keep the plants' natural form in mind, but always remove the following:

- broken or dead branches
- branches that cross or rub against each other, or are growing inward
- suckers arising from the base of the main stem
- dead needles that collect in the plant's interior

For information on what to do about diseased branches, see page 26.

Unlike most deciduous trees, many conifers have few or no *latent* buds on wood that is more than a couple of years old. (Latent buds are dormant buds that lie under the bark and will sprout if the terminal bud on the limb is removed.) Head back a huge old limb of a crabapple (*Malus*), and new shoots appear overnight. Cut to old wood on a modest limb of an eastern white pine (*Pinus strobus*), and the branch section you leave not only doesn't produce new growth, it dies. Conifers with whorled limbs tend to have fewer latent buds on old wood, but arborvitaes (*Thuja*), which have random branching, are notorious for refusing to produce new growth if you cut back too far.

Junipers (*Juniperus*), hemlocks (*Tsuga*), yews (*Taxus*), and redwoods (*Sequoia*) are among the evergreens that do have latent buds on older wood, but the results of pruning back that far are precarious. Cutting into old wood is unpredictable with so many conifers that removing entire branches back to the main stem—making a *thinning* cut—is recommended over *heading*, removing a portion of a large branch. Moreover, thinning preserves a tree's natural shape better than heading does. If you

Three Techniques for Pruning Conifers

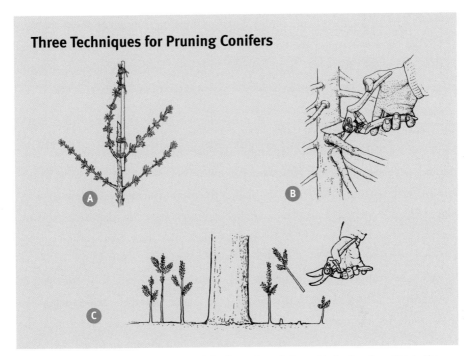

A: If the central leader gets damaged, cut it back to a lateral stem, attach a bamboo stick to the leader and bend up a strong lateral branch. B: Cut off crossing branches. C: Remove root suckers.

must head a limb, aim to leave a portion of limb that has green needles, or cut to another branch.

It's a mistake to prune an unhealthy plant, or to prune at a time of year when insects and diseases of conifers are active. All the standard rules for pruning deciduous plants also apply to conifers:

- Use clean, sharp tools; disinfect tools before moving between plants—even between limbs on a diseased plant (to disinfect, soak tools in a 10 percent bleach solution for one to two minutes).
- Use hedge shears only for shearing jobs, not for pruning.
- Always cut to a bud, a lateral branch, or the main trunk.
- Don't leave stubs, which are entry points for pathogens.
- If you make a pruning cut back to either the main stem or another branch, make sure you cut outside the raised branch collar, not flush to the wood you're cutting to. The collar contains chemicals that protect the tree against pathogens that can enter through the pruning wound. The sealing callus tissue will form a visible ring around the wound, a sign that it is closing properly. (For more about pruning cuts, see "The Kindest Cuts," page 18.)
- Don't apply pruning paints to wounds—they actually delay the closing of the wound.

• Prune in dry weather; many conifer diseases are spread by water-borne spores.

Not all conifers respond the same way to being pruned, nor do different species in the same genus. Before you begin lopping or sawing, remember this adage: Think twice, cut once. As pruning mavens like to say, you can't cut a limb back on.

Pruning Young Conifers

Most conifers either are sold balled and burlapped or are grown in containers, so no pruning beyond removing dead or damaged limbs is needed when you plant. (If diseased growth is obvious, don't buy the plant!) To ensure your conifers will be as spire-like as Frost's were, they must have one, strong *central leader*, or main stem. If competition appears, either remove it—by cutting the branch back to the central stem—or suppress the branch by weighting it so that it grows more out than up. (Any sort of weight you can tie to the limb works.) Sometimes central leaders are damaged. If that occurs, cut the leader back to a lateral stem, attach a sturdy bamboo stick to the leader with ties, then bend up a lateral branch—pick the strongest branch near the top—and tie it to the bamboo. (If a new, vigorous bud sprouts from the cut, allow it to serve as the new leader.)

The growth of many conifers, especially pines (*Pinus*), firs (*Abies*), and spruces (*Picea*), can be slowed by snapping or pinching off the emerging new tip growth. On pines, the shoot is known as a *candle*, and snapping it by a third or half is called *candling*. In addition to reducing growth, candling increases plant density by encouraging new shoots.

All the scaffold branches on a whorled conifer must remain in proportion to the main stem and to each other for the plant to be symmetrical. The best path to symmetricality is to pinch back overvigorous new shoots in spring. Do as little pruning as possible, for it may be difficult to conceal the loss of an entire limb. Errant branches can sometimes be weighted to grow in the direction or at the angle you want. Start at the top and work down, and step back frequently so you can see what you're doing.

Young conifers with random branching and less symmetricality are more easily pruned. You can limit size or promote bushy growth by heading back limbs (cut to a side branch) as well as by pinching back new growth. If you remove a portion of branch, try to make the cut so that it will be hidden by an overlapping branch. Don't forget that you can train as well as prune. Young branches will put up with a good deal of bending and directing. Training may take several years, but tying or weighting limbs to grow in the direction you want is nearly always preferable to lopping them off.

Pruning Old Conifers

Removing dead and damaged limbs of mature conifers is de rigueur but can be tricky. Branches and foliage of some species can appear dead when they're not. (The popular American arborvitae cultivar *Thuja occidentalis* 'Filiformis' turns brown in winter.) If you're not

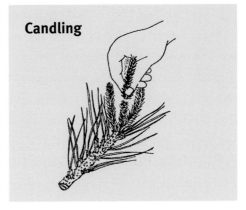

Candling

The growth of many conifers can be slowed by pinching off the emerging new tip growth.

sure that the limb has departed this world, wait until spring when new growth begins. Watch, too, for overcrowding, which is common in conifers. Without enough light, limbs decline and die.

The bottom branches of conifers frequently die back because of shading from upper growth and should be removed. You even may want to remove live branches at the bottom of a tree—called *lifting*—in order to protect a vista, to underplant, or to reveal ornamental bark like that of the Japanese red pine (*Pinus densiflora*) or the lace-bark pine (*P. bungeana*). If you're removing many limbs—and much foliage—space the cuts over several seasons.

Whenever you prune, either cut back to a bud, the base of a branch, or the main stem, taking care not to cut into the branch collar. Before you cut to a bud, see which direction it is pointing: New growth will grow in that direction. A bud pointing to the left will produce a stem that grows to the left. Above all, don't head back into the dreaded *dead zone*, the inner portion of conifer limbs—the section of old wood where there are no longer any green needles. There are exceptions, but many conifers have no or few latent buds in this region. If you cut back into the dead zone, the limb is unlikely to sprout new growth. It is likely to die. Thin the entire limb instead.

When you're removing a large limb, anything more than two inches in diameter, use a three-step cut to avoid damaging the bark on the tree. First, cut about halfway through the limb from beneath, 6 to 12 inches from the branch or trunk you're cutting to. Next, saw through the limb from the top, one to three inches beyond the first cut, until the limb falls. Last, remove the stub, cutting on a slight angle (from top out to bottom) just outside the branch collar. (Details about pruning techniques are in "The Kindest Cuts," page 18.)

Mature conifers, like youthful ones, respond to training; redirecting a limb is better than removing it. It may take several years before the limb acquiesces to its new position, so be patient. Weeping species, like weeping hemlock, *Tsuga canadensis* 'Pendula', are more likely to need support than pruning; lopsided trees can be staked to regain good posture. Train where necessary but try to take your marching orders from the tree and let it follow its natural form as much as possible.

A Plant-by-Plant Guide to Pruning Conifers

This partial list of conifers represents scores of species and cultivars, trees and shrubs, tall and ground-hugging, narrow and broad—and a palette of foliage colors, from yellow and gray through blue and darkest green. Before you begin cutting or sawing, remind yourself that most conifers want little or no pruning.

Abies species, firs. Firs are naturally pyramidal with whorled limbs and have some latent buds on old wood. Their soft needles are naturally dense; plants need only minimal pruning. Head errant branches back to a lateral, or thin to the main stem. Prune to a single leader; if the leader is damaged, cut back to healthy wood and allow a new shoot to form the new leader. Prune in early spring or as new growth emerges.

Cedrus species, cedars. True cedars have randomly spaced branches. Branches have spurs—short, stubby subbranches that contain some latent buds. To limit size, head back to a live bud or another limb. To produce a bushy plant, cut new shoots by one half in spring. Prune to a central leader; remove deadwood. Large wounds are slow to close up. *Cedrus deodara*, deodar cedar, is used as a hedge plant.

Chamaecyparis species, false cypresses, white cedars. False cypresses, which are randomly branched and have scalelike foliage, are famous for absolutely refusing to produce new growth on old wood; head back only to another branch or to a live bud. Plants tolerate shearing well. *Chamaecyparis thyoides,* Atlantic white cedar, and *C. nootkatensis,* Alaska cedar, are often used as hedge plants. Prune to a single leader. Pinch back stem ends to encourage dense growth.

Cupressus species, cypresses. Cypresses are randomly branched with scalelike and overlapping foliage; latent buds are hard to see. Prune to a single leader. Do not cut into the dead zone, the point beyond which a limb has no leaves. To encourage dense growth, head back branch tips. Cypresses are used as hedge plants.

Juniperus species, junipers, red cedars. Junipers, which have scalelike or needle leaves depending on the species, have randomly spaced limbs. They grow continuously throughout the garden season, and new growth is not obvious. Pinch stem ends or head back branches (to another branch) to limit size and encourage bushy growth. Prune anytime except when wood is frozen, although the best time is spring. Mature wood has some latent buds; needle species are less likely to produce new foliage on old wood.

Larix species, larches, tamaracks, hackmatacks. Larches, which are deciduous, have randomly spaced limbs; old wood has few dormant buds. To encourage fuller growth, pinch back new shoots in spring. When pruning limbs, cut to a live bud, another limb, or the main stem; do not cut into the dead zone. Prune to one central stem.

Picea species, spruces. Spruces have whorled limbs and some dormant buds on older wood. To control size, prune in early spring; always cut to a bud, side branch, or the main stem. Train to a single leader; do not head back the central leader. To encourage dense growth, cut back stem tips as they begin flushing. Remove bottom branches when they begin to die back.

Pinus species, pines. Pines flush in spring and should be pruned at that time. (A rule of thumb is to prune pines when the new needles reach half the length of mature needles.) Pines have whorled branches and no dormant buds on old wood. Prune to a single leader. To slow growth and promote density, snap back the candles by one third or one half with your fingers. To further control size, pinch out the central candle, which will stop growth. If necessary, remove entire limbs; do not head back limbs to old wood.

Pseudotsuga menziesii, Douglas fir. Needs little or no pruning. Branches are whorled and irregular and have few latent buds, so avoid heading back limbs to bare wood. Train to a single leader; shear stem tips in spring for dense growth. Can be used as a hedge plant. Do not top.

Sequoia sempervirens, sequoia, redwood. *Sequoia sempervirens* is randomly branched and has many latent buds. Train to a single leader; head or thin branches to control growth. Cut stem tips to encourage dense growth.

Sequoiadendron giganteum, **giant redwood.** Giant redwoods are randomly branching and have many latent buds. Train to a single leader. Remove suckers. Buy a very tall ladder.

Taxodium distichum, **bald cypress.** Bald cypresses have whorled branches, which have many latent buds and will tolerate severe pruning. Prune to a single leader. If planted near water, cypress knees, vertical conelike growths from the roots, will appear several feet from the tree.

Taxus **species, yews.** Yews are randomly branching and tolerant of severe pruning, which make them good hedge plants. Old wood contains many latent buds; even cuts in the dead zone will produce new growth. Control growth by thinning or heading; to encourage dense growth, cut back stem ends. Prune in spring before growth begins. Hedges can be sheared a second time in midsummer.

Thuja **species, arborvitaes, northern white cedars, swamp cedars.** Arborvitaes are randomly branching and have scalelike leaves. Train to a single leader; cuts in the dead zone—interior branch sections that lack needles—will not produce new growth. To encourage more density, cut back stem tips. Shear hedges after spring growth begins, then again in summer if needed.

Tsuga **species, hemlocks, hemlock spruces.** Hemlocks are randomly branched and flush many times during the growing season. They have a generous supply of latent buds on old wood. Train to a single leader. Hemlocks are often used as hedge plants; shear before growth begins in spring, again in midsummer. Remove entire limbs to retain the trees' natural shape.

Opposite: To preserve its natural look, individual branches were removed only as needed from this mountain pine, *Pinus mugo* 'Compacta', foreground. For a formal look, conifer shrubs can be shorn.

Vines and Climbers: Pruning Plants That Ascend

Vines are plants with long, long stems that make their way up in the world by clinging to or twining around a support. As long as there is something sturdy to mount, true vines can do it alone, or with minimal help. There are a handful of other plants that we call vines—*Bougainvillea* and climbing roses (*Rosa*) are two popular examples—that neither cling nor twine and can't ascend without help. Since they also want to be head and shoulders above their fellows, you must tie them to or drape them over a support.

As with other woody plants, the time and energy you'll spend pruning vines has much to do with the plant you select and the spot in which you place it. You'll save yourself a good deal of anguish if you pick a

Many vines just don't know when to quit—or in which direction to grow.

Grown as an annual in most regions, the tropical cypress vine, *Ipomoea quamoclit*, above, doesn't need much pruning. Most perennial vines, such as *Clematis* 'Comtesse de Bouchaud', opposite, need regular pruning to keep them healthy, productive, and under control.

vine that can live comfortably in the space you have. Old wisterias can produce primary stems the size of tree trunks and have been known to pry off drainpipes and gutters. Even my tropical wax plant (*Hoya carnosa*)—which hangs indoors and receives far less light than it needs—has managed to creep under the molding of the window, emerge on the other side, and now threatens to escape to the outdoors through a tiny tear in the screen.

How vines grow affects how much pruning they may need. Among the most intrepid are species that climb by using aerial rootlets and species like Virginia creeper (*Parthenocissus quinquefolia*) that have holdfasts, little suction cups that grab onto walls and other surfaces. Also exuberant (and sometimes invasive) are many vines that twine, such as *Wisteria*, bittersweet (*Celastrus scandens*), and honeysuckles (*Lonicera*). Somewhat less rampant are the vines that ascend by using tendrils, such as *Clematis*, grape (*Vitis*), and passionflower (*Passiflora*). But only somewhat.

Unlike many shrubs and trees that do well without ever being thinned or cut back, even vines grown in sizable settings may require regular pruning to keep them healthy, productive, attractive, and under control. Many vines just don't know when to quit— or in which direction to grow. They must be taken in hand early on or they will be collapsing trellises, pulling down fences, and obscuring windows and doors.

Once vines have developed adequate roots, most just keep on growing above ground. To keep a vigorous climber healthy, you must do the following:

- Remove any dead, damaged, diseased, or unproductive stems.
- Remove overly tangled stems.
- Remove errant stems, especially those growing away from the support.
- Direct its growth.
- Limit its growth.

Reducing a vine's mass not only ensures that your fence won't collapse, it also allows light and air to reach the plant's interior. Don't forget, though, that pruning doesn't just reduce mass: It can increase it. Heading back stems encourages new growth.

Vine-Pruning Primer

If you've purchased a container-grown vine—standard nursery fare these days—no pruning is mandatory at planting time, especially with evergreen vines. But heading back, which will encourage new growth, may be a good idea if your plant has long, spindly shoots with few leaves or only a single stem. Bare-root plants should be headed back by no more than a quarter before they are planted to allow the vine to balance its growth below and above ground. Be sure to cut out any damaged or dead roots

When to prune *Clematis* depends on what type it is. Prune *Clematis montana* var. *rubens*, left, after flowering. Prune *Clematis* 'General Sikorski', right, lightly in winter.

and stems, or stems that have minds of their own and appear determined to grow into the neighbor's yard rather than up your trellis.

Vines in their first or second year tend to sprout and elongate stems more than produce leaves and flowers. Pinching back shoot ends helps balance their growth. Also, woody vines tend to flower more generously on shoots that are horizontal rather than vertical, so keep that in mind as you direct and shape your climbers. Twining vines especially grow from upper buds and tend to lose their lower leaves. They may need severe heading back to promote foliage near the ground. If you want a compact vine, head back stems throughout the growing season; if you want a vine to ramble, keep your pruning shears in their scabbard.

The guidelines for pruning mature vines are similar to those for pruning deciduous shrubs. Species grown for their foliage can be pruned throughout the garden season, but early spring before leaves appear puts the least stress on the plant. Vines that flower in summer and fall on the current year's growth, such as honeysuckles (*Lonicera*), should be pruned in late winter or early spring. That schedule gives the plant time to produce new shoots and flowers. Prune vines that flower early in the garden season on shoots produced the previous year—jasmines (*Jasminum*) and *Wisteria* are two—immediately after their flowers fade. Most hardy vines fall into this category.

Except... like all general rules, there are exceptions, the most important of which concerns vines that produce ornamental or edible fruits. Even if postflowering pruning is called for, wait until spring, or the fruit crop will be lost.

Vine Maintenance Pruning

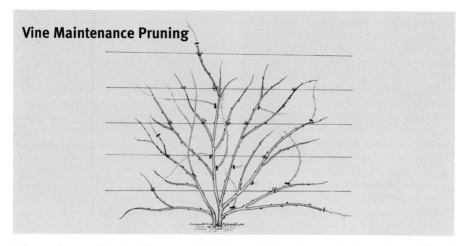

To keep a vigorous climber healthy, remove dead, damaged, diseased, unproductive, overly tangled, and errant stems, such as those shown in gray on this vine growing on horizontal supports.

When you prune, be sure to do the following:

- Cut to healthy wood if removing dead, diseased, or damaged growth.
- Cut back to a lateral shoot or bud.
- Cut to a bud or stem that is pointing in the direction you want the vine to go.
- Cut cleanly and don't leave a stub, which is an invitation to bugs and diseases.

Incense passionflower, *Passiflora* 'Incense', blooms on new wood and needs only moderate pruning unless it's grown for fruit production.

Pruning mature vines can be difficult, because their long stems become tangled. Don't be tempted to yank. Instead, prune one stem section at a time until you've cut out all you want to remove.

A Vine-by-Vine Guide to Pruning

Some vines don't *have* to be pruned every year, but all vines need basic care: Remove dead, damaged, and diseased stems; stems that are tangled or head in the wrong direction; stems that are weak or unproductive; unwanted suckers; and spent flowers. Beyond those cuts, the general goal when pruning vines is to keep them healthy, vigorous, and productive, and to help them follow their natural inclinations at the same time they fulfill your needs.

Actinidia species, kiwi, silver vine. Flower on new wood. Do maintenance pruning—to train or control—on silver vine (*Actinidia polygama*), variegated kiwi vine (*A. kolomikta*), and other ornamental actinidias after they flower. Save severe or renewal pruning for late winter to early spring when the vine is dormant.

Aristolochia macrophylla, Dutchman's pipe, pipevine. Dutchman's pipe flowers on old wood, but it is grown for its foliage and can be pruned anytime to remove tangles and errant shoots. Save renewal pruning for late winter to early spring when the vine is dormant, then cut oldest stems to six inches.

Bignonia capreolata, crossvine, quartervine, trumpet flower. Flowers on new wood. Prune to remove weak, overgrown, or errant shoots in late winter to early spring; head back shoots to encourage new growth. Needs minimal pruning.

Bougainvillea species, bougainvilleas, paper flowers. Most bougainvilleas flower intermittently throughout the year on new growth, with the heaviest bloom cycles (followed by a rest cycle) coming in spring and fall. Prune after flowering ends. Remove dead, tangled, and errant wood and suckers; head back long stems to encourage new flower buds.

Campsis radicans, trumpet creeper, trumpet vine, cow-itch. Flowers on new growth. Head back stems in late winter to early spring to control growth and encourage branching. Remove suckers and root-prune to discourage underground runners. Cut stems to ten inches to renew.

Celastrus scandens, American bittersweet. Blooms on new wood. Prune in late winter to early spring. Remove suckers, tangled and weak stems, and stems that have fruited; head back last year's growth; pinch shoot tips in summer to encourage branching. Do not confuse this native species with *Celastrus orbiculatus*, oriental bittersweet, which is invasive.

Clematis, clematis. See "Clematis: The Queen of Vines," page 74.

Cocculus carolinus, Carolina moonseed, coral beads. Flowers on new wood; prune as needed in early spring.

Ficus pumila, creeping fig, climbing fig. Remove older stems in late winter or early spring to promote immature foliage form. Pinch stem ends to promote branching. Needs little pruning.

Gelsemium sempervirens, Carolina jessamine, evening trumpet flower. Flowers on old wood. Head back lateral shoots, remove dead stems, and prune to shape after flowering ends.

Humulus lupulus, common hop. Flowers on new growth. Commercial growers cut their hop vines to the ground in late summer to harvest the cones. Hop vines grown for ornament should be cut to the ground in late winter to early spring. Root-prune to control underground runners.

Hydrangea petiolaris, climbing hydrangea. Flowers on new wood. Head back in early spring; remove stems that have pulled away from their support. Prune hard to renew.

Ipomoea species, cypress vine, morning glory. *Ipomoea* species, including morning glory (*I. tricolor*) and moonflower (*I. alba*), the p.m. version of the morning glory, flower on new wood. Cut vines to the ground in late winter to early spring in zones where they are perennial.

Jasminum nudiflorum, winter jasmine. Flowers on old wood; prune immediately after blooms fade. Winter jasmine, primrose jasmine (*Jasminum mesnyi*), and common, or poet's, jasmine (*J. officinale*) need minimal pruning.

Lonicera, honeysuckle. Prune Henry's honeysuckle (*Lonicera henryi*), trumpet honeysuckle (*L. sempervirens*), woodbine (*L. periclymenum*), and trumpet honeysuckle cultivars (*L.* × *brownii*) in late winter to early spring to control growth; remove weak shoots; head back long stems. Renew old vines by cutting a third of oldest stems to the ground. Japanese honeysuckle (*L. japonica*) and its cultivars are extremely invasive and not recommended.

Mandevilla splendens, mandevilla. Flowers throughout the growing season on old wood; little or no pruning necessary.

Menispermum canadense, Canada moonseed, yellow parilla. Flowers on new wood. Postpone pruning until spring to preserve ornamental fruits. Root-prune to control underground suckers.

Parthenocissus species. Most *Parthenocissus* species, including Virginia creeper, or woodbine (*P. quinquefolia*), and Boston ivy (*P. tricuspidata*), need pruning only to

Pruning mature vines such as this *Bougainvillea* can be difficult because their long stems become tangled. Don't be tempted to yank. Instead prune stems section by section.

control or direct their growth. Grown for their leaves, they can be shaped throughout the garden season; wait until late winter to early spring to do radical pruning.

Passiflora species, passionflowers. Bloom on new growth; remove tangled and unproductive stems in spring. Need only moderate pruning unless grown for fruit production.

Periploca graeca, silkvine. Flowers on new wood. Little pruning needed; head back in spring to stimulate and direct growth.

Rosa species and cultivars, climbing and rambling roses. See "Roses," page 76.

Schisandra species. *Schisandra* species, such as Chinese magnolia vine (*S. chinensis*) and bay star vine (*S. coccinea*), flower in spring on old wood, but postpone pruning until late winter or early spring to preserve their ornamental beaded fruits.

Schizophragma species, hydrangea vine. Both Japanese hydrangea vine (*Schizophragma hydrangeoides*) and *S. integrifolium* flower on new wood. Prune in early spring; little pruning is needed.

Vitis species, grapes. Flower on new growth. Grape species traditionally are pruned in late winter. Ornamental grapes, such as *V. vinifera* 'Brandt', *V. vinifera* 'Purpurea', and *V. coignetiae* do not require the careful and severe pruning that is needed when growing grapes for their fruits.

Wisteria species, wisteria. Native wisterias, including American wisteria (*W. frutescens*) and Kentucky wisteria (*W. macrostachya*), are less vigorous and showy than Asian species, which are invasive. They flower on short, leafy shoots, or

Clematis: The Queen of Vines

Clematis are among the most beautiful flowering vines but also among the most puzzling when it comes to pruning. Most flower without any pruning—at least for a few years—but if you wait too long, the severe pruning that may be necessary can be a death knell. All clematis benefit from being pinched back to the lowest pair of healthy buds when planted, and pinched again in their second season if growth is slow and stems sparse.

The key to pruning clematis safely and effectively is to know what class of vine you're growing. Once you know what you've got—another argument for saving the tags that come with plants—the rest is easy. The experts have divided the genus into three groups.

Group One, the spring-flowering clematis that bloom on old wood, should be pruned lightly after they blossom. Old, overly tall woody vines can be pruned hard, but it may take a season or two for them to recover.

Prune *Group Two*, the late- and twice-blooming clematis, which blossom on both old and new wood, lightly in late winter when the vine is dormant. After their first flowering, prune them more heavily—cut back about a third of the shoots to the lowest pair of healthy buds—to induce new growth for fall flowers.

Group Three, the late-flowering clematis, which bloom on new wood, should be cut back to the lowest pair of healthy buds in late winter to early spring, before new growth begins.

Clematis Group One	Clematis Group Two	Clematis Group Three
C. alpina, alpine clematis	*C. florida*	*C. tanguitica*, Russian virgin's bower
C. macropetala	*C.* 'Barbara Jackman'	*C. terniflora*, sweet autumn clematis
C. montana	*C.* 'Duchess of Edinburgh'	
C. spooneri	*C.* 'Empress of India'	*C. texensis*, scarlet clematis
C. 'Apple Blossom'	*C.* 'Fairy Queen'	*C. viticella*
C. 'Blue Bird'	*C.* 'General Sikorski'	*C.* 'Comtesse de Bouchaud'
C. 'Crimson Star'	*C.* 'Henryi'	*C.* 'Ernest Markham'
C. 'Rubens'	*C.* 'Mme. le Coutre'	*C.* 'Gravetye Beauty'
C. 'Snowdrift'	*C.* 'Nelly Moser'	*C.* 'Huldine'
	C. 'Prince of Wales'	*C.* 'Jackmanii'
	C. 'The President'	*C.* 'Perle d'Azur'
	C. 'Vyvyan Pennel'	*C.* 'Warsaw Nike'

pedicels, that arise from buds on the previous year's wood. To encourage flowering, head back stems after blooms have faded; if necessary, head back a second time in late winter, leaving at least three or four buds. Train shoots to establish a framework or increase vine height; head back once the desired height and width have been achieved. Old plants can be renewed by severe pruning, almost to the ground.

Late-flowering *Clematis texensis* blooms on new wood and should be cut back to the lowest pair of healthy buds in late winter or early spring, before new growth begins.

Roses: Pruning the Sweetest Flower

All roses (*Rosa*) benefit from some pruning, and some roses benefit from lots of pruning. Remember, roses are not unique: They are deciduous shrubs, and they respond to being snipped and sawed the same way many other shrubs

> "A rose is a rose is a rose except when it comes to pruning."

do. Whatever roses you're growing, the goal when pruning is to keep your plants healthy; to control and shape growth; and to encourage the development of flowering wood.

Getting to know your roses is important. Different types of roses require different treatments. (As one wit put it, "A rose is a rose is a rose except when it comes to pruning.") As a general rule, the nearer your rosebush is to being a species, the less pruning it will need. 'Kaiserin Auguste Viktoria', a proud white hybrid tea that's been around since 1891, and 'Whisper', a new white hybrid tea rose from Ireland and a 2003 All-America Rose Selections winner, will both need more care than *Rosa virginiana*.

It's not easy to kill a rose with pruners. Despite the glorious delicacy of their flowers and fragrances, roses are a hardy lot. However, plants that are never pruned become a tangle of increasingly smaller canes that eventually bloom on the end of woody stalks; they also attract more than their share of diseases and insects. Unlike tree

Opposite: Give climbers and ramblers such as *Rosa* 'Excelsa' a few years to get established before you start pruning.

trunks, which just keep growing, most rose canes weaken—sometimes after only three or four years—and should be removed, or at least severely headed back. A rose plant may live 50 years—the record holder is a dog rose (*Rosa canina*) in Hildesheim, Germany, planted in the ninth century—but its individual stems tend to die young.

Bark color is one guide to the age of your rose's canes. New, vigorous growth is either red or green; older wood is very dark green or brown and often scaly. Not all roses show their age by the color of their canes, but pith, the center of the cane, never lies. The pith of a healthy cane is light tan or white. Brown pith signals a dead or diseased cane, one that should be headed back or removed.

As you prune, you're encouraging new growth, including the formation of flower-bearing side or lateral stems. If your rose has a healthy root system, regrowth will be quick. Severe pruning, remember, stimulates more growth than light pruning does, but it's harder on the plant. It also yields fewer—albeit larger—flowers. If exhibition roses—flowers the size of dinner plates—are the goal, cut away; otherwise, think of renewal as the pruning goal, keeping your plant healthy and vigorous. (See "The Why and When of Pruning," page 6, for more about the effects of pruning.)

The Appointed Hour

When you prune depends on which roses you're growing and on where you live. Most modern roses bloom continuously or more than once during the garden season. These roses flower on new lateral or sublateral stems, so the lion's share of pruning occurs in spring, or as soon as the buds on the canes begin to swell but before they break. If you prune too early, the new shoots will be vulnerable to late frosts. If you wait until new growth is well under way, you stress the plants by forcing them to produce stems and leaves twice in a short span of time. You should also avoid pruning in late summer or fall, as it stimulates new growth that won't have time to harden off and will likely be killed in winter.

When to Prune Roses

"Prune roses when the forsythia blooms." That's phenological wisdom, the use of events in the life cycles of plants and animals to time garden activities such as planting and harvesting. Phenological sayings—"When the dogwood flowers appear, frost will not again be here"—were followed long before the National Oceanic and Atmospheric Administration began handing out advice. And you don't just prune when the forsythia blooms; this is also the time to fertilize roses. Just remember that phenological advice is site specific. When the buds on 'Peace' begin to swell, forsythia or no, it's time to prune.

Rosa wichuraiana, a species rose, needs only maintenance pruning after flowering.

Gardeners living in colder climates prune far more judiciously than their compatriots in the South. Their garden season is shorter and cooler, and their plants suffer more winterkill. After a northern gardener removes dead wood in spring, it's likely that no additional structural pruning is necessary. Northern gardeners should keep their rosebushes relatively tall—longer canes produce more flowers earlier, an advantage in a short growing season. However, in areas where winter winds are severe, it is advisable to cut back stems sufficiently in early winter to protect the roots from loosening. (It may also be necessary to cover more delicate roses such as floribundas and hybrid teas with evergreen bows or loosely surround them with straw in a wire basket built around the rose.) In mild climates, long canes may survive winter without damage, but gardeners sometimes must prune simply to keep their roses in bounds.

Matters of Course

You'll want to wear leather gloves when you prune roses. Use sharp, clean-cutting bypass pruning shears (not anvil pruners, which crush stems). If your roses are old and have stems greater than half an inch in diameter, you'll also need a small pruning saw or a pair of loppers. (For more on tools, see "Outfitting the Pruner," page 100.) Every cut needs to be clean—don't leave jagged edges or stubs. To avoid spreading disease problems, dip your tools in a 10 percent bleach solution or in isopropyl alcohol before you move from one rose to the next.

With roses purchased bare-root, it's usually a good idea to remove any damaged or dead roots and stems, and head the top growth back to about a foot (remove only damaged or dead stems of climbers and standards) at planting time. Container-grown roses need minimal pruning at this time: Remove damaged or dead wood, and if you want, cut stem tips back to the next-highest bud.

For established roses, do the following before pruning for structure and flowering:

- Remove canes that are dead, dying, or diseased.
- Head back damaged canes.
- Remove any suckers sprouting from the rootstock of grafted roses.
- Remove inward-growing and crossing canes.
- Remove extremely old, gnarled, and woody canes.
- Remove canes that are weak, twiggy, or very thin ("thinner than a pencil" is the usual measure for hybrid tea roses).
- Remove nonflowering canes. (On roses that bloom on old wood be careful not to confuse them with young canes that may produce flowers in future years).
- Deadhead repeat and continuous bloomers (but not roses with decorative hips).

When making pruning cuts, try to follow these guidelines:

- Strive to "open" the plant so that light and air can reach its center.
- Always cut to an outward-facing bud—cut a quarter of an inch above the bud, slanted away from the bud.
- Make sure you cut to live wood.
- Don't leave stubs.
- Use your thumb and forefinger to remove all but one bud if there are several buds emerging at your cut.

Cutting a bouquet is also a form of pruning. Don't cut roses from frail plants. On healthy plants, cut the stem to a leaf with five or seven leaflets, leaving *at least* two leaf shoots on the stem.

Know Your Roses

Before you start pruning, identify what kind of rose you're growing. If you know the cultivar name it's easy to track down

Rosa 'Peace' is a hybrid tea, a repeat-flowering rose that should be deadheaded regularly.

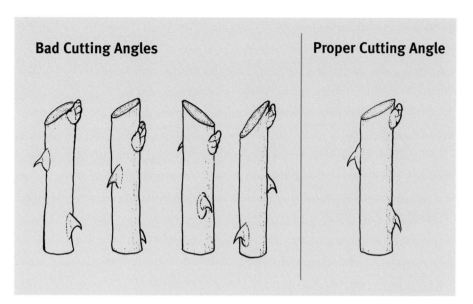

Bad Cutting Angles | **Proper Cutting Angle**

When pruning roses, every cut needs to be clean. Don't leave jagged edges, and be sure to angle your cut just above and away from the nearest bud at a 45-degree angle, as shown above on the far right.

its class. (*The Handbook for Selecting Roses*, published each year by the American Rose Society, is the official word, but there are thousands of rose resources, both in print and online.) The ARS's classification scheme reflects "the botanical and evolutionary progress of the rose." It collects roses into three groups: species, or wild roses; old garden roses—classes in existence before 1867; and modern roses—post-1867 classes.

Altogether there are now 35 official rose classes. For pruning purposes it's easier to think of five general groups: species roses, old garden roses, modern roses, ramblers, and climbers. These are functional aggregations. What's important is that you prune at the right time in the right way. (For more details on the requirements of individual roses, see "For More Information," page 110.)

Species Roses occur naturally throughout the Northern Hemisphere. Many of the approximately 125 "unimproved" or wild roses thrive with little help in the garden, as long as you plant them in a suitable location and give them room to grow. Species roses, which rarely flower more than once a season, usually need only maintenance pruning, and the best time for it is right after flowering. Removing old canes is the best way to renew many species roses, but don't remove more than a third of the plant at one time.

Old Garden Roses rarely need hard pruning; allow new plants a couple of seasons to become established before going in with the shears. For pruning purposes, old garden roses can be divided into one-time bloomers and repeat bloomers.

Cultivars that bloom only once during the garden season—most of the alba, damask, centifolia, gallica, and moss roses—blossom on old wood. To reduce density, prune immediately after flowering ends by removing a few of the least productive canes each year.

Old garden roses that are repeat bloomers, such as Bourbons, hybrid perpetuals, Portlands, and Noisettes, flower on both old and new wood. Prune in spring, before the buds open, then deadhead after the first flowering ends to produce a second round of blooms. Remove a few of the oldest canes each year to promote new growth; head back the remaining canes by a fourth or a third, leaving at least three to four healthy buds per cane. As with all repeat bloomers, deadhead by cutting back the stem to the first leaf with five or seven leaflets below the spent blossom.

Modern Roses make up a catchall group, which includes everything from hybrid musks like 'Ballerina' and 'Felicia' to the *R. kordesii* hybrids like 'William Baffin', *R. rugosa* hybrids like 'Sir Thomas Lipton', floribundas, grandifloras, polyanthas, and hybrid teas, as well as modern shrub roses including the Meidiland cultivars, Explorer roses, and Morden/Parkland roses. Some of the most popular modern shrub roses are cultivars introduced by English breeder David Austin, usually listed as English roses. Most shrub roses are the result of breeders' attempts to create roses

for landscape use—continuously blooming roses that have disease-resistant foliage and good hardiness. Shrub roses don't need heavy pruning.

Give new plants a chance to become established before pruning. After a year or two, prune in spring before the buds open. Remove weak, thin canes. Head back the canes of roses with an upright habit by a third to encourage new laterals; prune spreading types less severely. Don't remove new basal shoots growing from the graft union—they become new

Apothecary's rose, *Rosa gallica* 'Officinalis', is an old garden rose, and as such rarely needs hard pruning.

Be sure not to deadhead roses with attractive hips, such as *Rosa rugosa*.

flowering canes. But do keep your eye out for suckers, which arise from *below* the graft union. Watch for basal canes with leaves that look different from the rest of the rose's leaves. If possible, gently *pull* the shoots off; cutting them can encourage the development of even more suckers. Every year or two, thin out a portion of the oldest canes. To avoid trouble with rebellious rootstocks, look for roses grown on their own roots.

Polyanthas, floribundas, grandifloras, and hybrid teas are usually repeat-flowering, or remontant, and are pruned in early spring before their buds break. The general rule is moderate pruning for more flowers earlier, severe pruning for fewer (but bigger) flowers later. Modern reflowering roses, which bloom on old and new wood, should be deadheaded regularly. It's also important to keep the center of cultivars with an upright form open. With all these roses, open the plant by cutting to outward-facing buds.

Polyantha roses like 'The Fairy' and 'Cécile Brunner' are regaining some of their former popularity. Generally, polyanthas flower continuously, and many make first-rate patio plants. Give your plant a year to become established. The following spring, cut the one-year canes back by a third; the next spring, cut those canes back by a half to two thirds. Polyanthas produce many spindly basal shoots; from the third year on, keep the thickest, strongest canes and remove the rest.

Floribunda roses, such as 'Livin' Easy' and 'Sunsprite', are the largest class of roses after hybrid teas and produce clusters of blossoms throughout summer and into fall. Hard prune new plants, cutting canes back to four to six buds. Once the structure is established, prune in early spring by opening the center, heading back the main canes by about a third to half, and pruning lateral shoots to two to three buds (the older the plant, the more vigorously you can prune). Prune old, unproductive canes to six inches. In cold climates, leave as much live growth as possible.

Grandiflora roses, nearly all of which are grafted, are crosses between hybrid tea and floribunda roses. The result? Tea-rose-like blooms, usually produced in clusters, with strong stems. Most cultivars rebloom well if deadheaded promptly. Prune new plants to about one foot, and in the second year, gently prune for structure. Prune grandifloras such as 'Aquarius' and 'Camelot' in early spring. Remove spindly and unproductive stems, then head back the vigorous main canes to 18 to 24 inches. Head lateral shoots to two to three buds. Prune more gently in cold regions.

Hybrid tea roses like 'Tropicana' and 'Medallion' usually produce only one flower per stem, but what a flower it is! The first hybrid tea, 'La France', appeared in 1867, and the breeders haven't taken a day off since. Some hybrid teas may not be the sweetest roses—although breeders are beginning to catch on that roses should smell good—but nothing beats them for the size, color, and form of their flowers. If you want to exhibit roses, consult a local rosarian about pruning. For everyday gardeners, life is easier.

New plants should be pruned hard: Cut back to a foot or less, leaving three to six buds per cane. Prune gently the second year for structure. Prune established roses in spring. How severely you cut depends on the cultivar you're growing. The general rule is to head canes back by about a third to half. Some gardeners remove all lateral shoots; others leave the strongest. It's your call. But do remove any weak, spindly stems that won't produce flowers, anything smaller in diameter than a pencil. Always cut back to an outside bud, which will keep the center of the rose open to air and sun.

Even if they don't exhibit their hybrid tea roses some gardeners disbud them—remove the small lateral flower buds so that all the plant's energy goes to a single remaining bud. In northern climates, disbudding isn't recommended. A mandatory practice for gardeners everywhere is watching for suckers. Many hybrid tea roses are grafted and may send up suckers from their rootstock, below the graft union. Remove them by pulling, not cutting, if possible. And don't forget to deadhead hybrid teas, cutting back stems to the first set of five or seven leaflets as soon as the flower petals begin to drop. With hybrid tea roses and all repeat-flowering roses, deadheading *is*

pruning, essential to pro-
longing their blooming.

Ramblers and Climbers

All roses with aspirations to
rise above their companions
need more than assistance
in their ascent—they must
be tied to or draped over a
support—they also require
some pruning to remain
productive and healthy. Fan
the canes so that they produce flower-bearing laterals
along their entire length;
vertical canes tend to produce blooms only at the tips
of their stems. Give this
group of roses—whether
they're called climbers or

Rosa 'Blush Noisette' can be grown as a shrub or a climber. At pruning time be sure to remove trailing stems section by section to avoid damaging the stems you are leaving.

ramblers—a couple of years to become established before you prune. Then how you
prune depends on the type of rose you're growing. In any case, when pruning ascending
roses, remove stems in sections so you don't damage the stems you're leaving. Climbing
roses are usually pruned according to their habit.

Ramblers—identified by their long, flexible canes—should be trained as soon as flowering ends. Tie in new growth and train the rose to its supporting structure. Ramblers like
'American Pillar', 'Excelsa', and 'Dorothy Perkins' send up new canes from the base each
year and blossom on those that are at least a year old. In spring, tie in the canes which
should remain and cut out old canes that are no longer productive; head back lateral
shoots to three to six inches on the remaining canes, leaving three to four buds per shoot.

The so-called rampant ramblers like 'Wedding Day' and 'Francis E. Lester' need
only maintenance pruning. Remove any unproductive canes. Deadhead during
blooming season and train new growth. In spring, cut back laterals by two thirds and
maintain structure.

Climbers such as 'Paul's Scarlet Climber' and 'Albéric Barbier' do not send up many
new shoots from the base every year. Train and tie in the existing canes to their support-

Deadheading

Deadheading—removing wilted flowers—keeps roses from forming hips, the red fruits that contain seeds. Some roses, mostly one-time bloomers like *R. rugosa* and *R. moyesii*, produce such gorgeous hips that you'll want to let them develop. With reblooming cultivars, such as hybrid teas, deadheading encourages the rose to put all its efforts into producing more flowers. To deadhead, cut to the next outward-facing bud or leaf with five leaflets, just as the petals begin to drop.

Roses produce leaves with three, five, and seven leaflets. Early in the summer and on weak plants, the first stems will probably have only leaves with three leaflets. Cut to them. Later and on strong plants, cut to five-leaflet clusters. You can prune farther down the stem than the next leaf. The aim is to cut back far enough so that the new growth will be floriferous without depleting the plant. Cut at a 45-degree angle just above the node. To avoid winterkill, northern gardeners stop deadheading about six weeks before the fall frost date.

Modern shrub roses, such as the *R. kordesii* hybrid 'William Baffin', were bred for easy maintenance. Once established, these roses are pruned in early spring before the buds open.

ing structure and cut back flowering laterals to three or four buds. Be sure to save strong new canes coming from the base; they are necessary for plant structure and renewal.

Repeat-flowering climbers bloom on new lateral shoots growing from old wood. Deadhead them after flowering to encourage more flowers. Tie in and train strong new growth and, depending on the vigor of the plant, cut back laterals of 'Climbing Iceberg', 'Handel', 'Mermaid', 'Meg', and other repeat-flowering climbers by up to half. In early spring, cut back flowering laterals to three or four buds. Shape and tie in frame canes and stronger new growth to the supporting structure.

Roses by Pruning Group

Following are short lists of some popular rose species and cultivars, grouped according to the five basic pruning groups discussed above.

Species Roses

R. banksiae, Lady Bank's rose

R. carolina, pasture rose

R. eglanteria, sweetbriar rose

R. foetida 'Bicolor', Austrian copper

R. glauca, red-leaf rose

R. rugosa, rugosa rose

R. spinosissima, Scotch rose

R. wichuraiana, memorial rose

Old Garden Roses

R. 'Mutabilis' China

R. 'Baronne Prévost', repeat-flowering

R. 'Céleste', alba

R. 'Harison's Yellow', hybrid foetida

R. 'Mme. Hardy', damask

R. 'Officinalis' (apothecary's rose), gallica

R. 'Stanwell Perpetual', hybrid *spinosissima,* repeat-flowering

R. 'Zéphirine Drouhin', Bourbon, repeat-flowering

Modern Roses

R. 'Abraham Darby', modern shrub

R. 'Carefree Wonder', modern shrub

R. 'Color Magic', hybrid tea

R. 'Delicata', hybrid rugosa

R. 'Elizabeth Taylor', hybrid tea

R. 'French Lace', floribunda

R. 'Gold Medal', grandiflora

R. 'Graham Thomas', modern shrub

R. 'Hansa', hybrid rugosa

R. 'Knockout', modern shrub

R. 'Morden Pink', modern shrub

R. 'Olé', grandiflora

R. 'Peace', hybrid tea

R. 'Queen Elizabeth', grandiflora

R. 'Sally Holmes', modern shrub

R. 'Scentimental', floribunda

R. 'Sir Thomas Lipton', hybrid rugosa

R. 'Trumpeter', floribunda

R. 'White Meidiland', modern shrub

Climbers

R. 'Altissimo', repeat-flowering climber

R. 'Clair Matin', repeat-flowering climber

R. 'Don Juan', repeat-flowering climber

R. 'Dr. W. Van Fleet', climber

R. 'Joseph's Coat', repeat-flowering climber

Ramblers

R. 'Ayrshire Splendens', rambler

R. 'Chevy Chase', rambler

R. 'Dorothy Perkins', rambler

R. 'Excelsa', rambler

R. 'Paul's Himalayan Musk', rambler

Special Cases: Pruning for Particular Purposes

Bonsai—the ultimate in pruning magic—is usually an indoor horticultural sport and beyond the scope of this book. (For more information, consult Brooklyn Botanic Garden handbooks *Indoor Bonsai* and *Bonsai Special Techniques*.) However, there are other more-challenging-than-usual pruning enterprises that may find a place in your garden. Before planting a hedge or starting a topiary, just remember that these pruning undertakings take time and perseverance. They probably aren't for the casual gardener.

Hedges

No hedge will be successful unless you've chosen a plant or combination of plants that can fulfill your screening needs. Evergreen species with small or medium leaves such as boxwoods (*Buxus*) are best for formal hedges, as are many conifers, including eastern red cedar and Rocky Mountain juniper (*Juniperus virginiana, J. scopulorum*), yews (*Taxus*), arborvitaes (*Thuja*), and hemlocks (*Tsuga*).

Almost any shrub or small tree can be part of an informal hedge that is pruned minimally, just enough to ensure dense growth, to control size, and to promote good health. Lilacs (*Syringa*), species and old garden roses (*Rosa*), Virginia sweetspire (*Itea virginica*), hawthorns (*Crataegus*), witch alder (*Fothergilla*), alpine currant (*Ribes alpinum*), flowering quinces (*Chaenomeles*), and cinquefoils (*Potentilla*) are a few

Pleaching involves weaving tree branches together to form arbors, screens, arches, lattices, and other structures. At right is an allée of pleached beech trees.

As with other plants, when pruning a hedge, remove damaged and dead wood first, then prune for shape and size.

good deciduous choices. Conifers, hollies (*Ilex*), and mountain laurel (*Kalmia latifolia*) can be used as well. You can reduce maintenance by choosing plants that will require less pruning, such as hollies, spruces (*Picea*), and hornbeams (*Carpinus*).

Young hedge plants should be pruned after the first year of growth. In early spring of the second year, remove half of the new growth on deciduous plants, especially if you have a formal hedge in mind, and do that again in the third year. Then begin to shape the hedge. Don't head back new conifers; instead, begin to shape them gently after they've been in the ground for a year or three. Once an informal hedge is estab-

Proper Shapes for Formal Hedges

Formal, sheared hedges should be wider at the bottom and narrower at the top to allow sunlight to reach lower branches (A), which otherwise would become bare and unsightly (C). In regions with heavy snowfall, hedges with broad flat tops (B, left) may be damaged by the weight of excessive snow accumulation. Hedges clipped in straight lines (B, center) require frequent trimming. Rounded forms (B, right) hinder snow accumulation and require less trimming.

lished, it shouldn't require much more than maintenance pruning; formal hedges need more care. New England nurseryman and author Lewis Hill believes the best advice for pruning hedges is, "Do it when they look like they need it."

Formal or informal, the most important thing to know about maintaining a healthy hedge is that it *must* be wider at the bottom than at the top—in other words, shaped like an upside-down V. (This ensures that the bottom branches don't die from being shaded by upper branches.) The top of the hedge can be rounded or flat, but snowbelt gardeners will want to keep it fairly narrow.

Radical Hedge Surgery

An overgrown, barebottomed hedge—decrepit and ugly—is practically a given when you buy an old house in some parts of the country. If you want to retain it, and it's a deciduous hedge, take a chance and cut it back severely, both in height and width, in early spring. Then begin shaping it as new growth appears, making sure that shoots grow outward. Evergreen hedges are more difficult. Most conifers don't come back from radical pruning. (Yews are one exception.) Deciduous or coniferous, taming a badly overgrown hedge is always dicey. Don't be too surprised if renovation turns into replacement.

Informal hedges require only a good pair of pruning shears or loppers, as they need only to be trimmed to encourage dense growth and to limit height. For a formal hedge, you'll need hedge shears. And string and stakes and a level. Trust the experts on this one: If you want a straight, uniform hedge, you must do more than eyeball it. String lines, test with a level, and trust that bubble no matter what your eye tells you.

As with other plants, do maintenance work first—remove damaged and dead wood—then prune your hedge for shape and size. The best time to prune conifer hedges is early spring, before the plants break bud, then again in midsummer. That timing ensures that the cuts you make will be quickly hidden by new growth. (For specific information about pruning conifers, see page 54.) Deciduous hedges should be pruned according to the special needs of the plants you're using, especially if you've planted flowering or fruiting species. (For specific information on deciduous shrubs and trees, see "Shrubs," page 28, and "Deciduous Trees," page 40.)

Topiary

Topiary—trees, shrubs, and vines transformed into balls, corkscrews, elephants, and more—requires more than a good pair of hedge shears. It requires the right plant, better-than-average growing conditions, lots of time, the patience of Job, and a good

Topiary Shapes

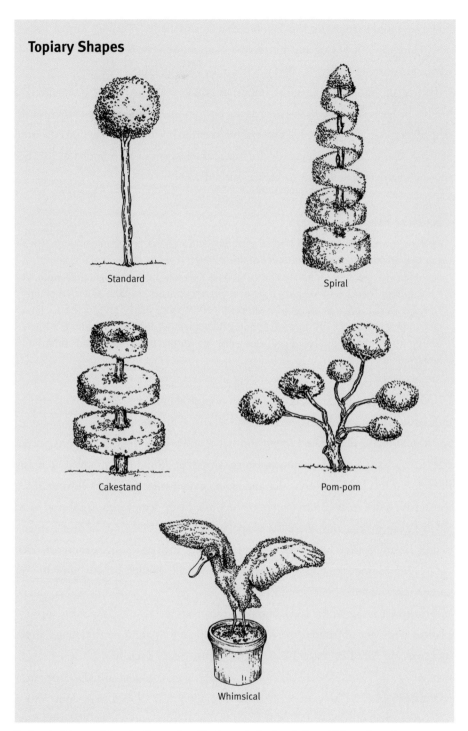

Standard

Spiral

Cakestand

Pom-pom

Whimsical

Topiary is living sculpture for the garden: Plants are trained and clipped into various shapes. Species with tight, slow growth and small foliage that can withstand constant and heavy pruning are ideal topiary plants.

Training a Standard

Often grown in a container, the *standard* is a topiary with a single stem topped by a globe of foliage. A botanical lollipop. To create a standard, begin with a young plant. Remove all basal stems but one—it will become the trunk—and stake it to keep it straight. Pinch back (but don't remove) shoots growing from the main stem. Once the plant reaches the height you want, pinch out its terminal bud. Form the head by pinching side shoots as soon as they grow a few inches. Last, bare the trunk by removing shoots growing from the lower portion of the main stem. Once established, standards need only occasional maintenance pruning. Following are suggested candidates for potted standards.

Bougainvillea × *buttiana*, bougainvillea

Camellia species, camellias

Gardenia species, gardenias

Laurus nobilis, bay laurel

Myrtus communis, myrtle

Rosmarinus officinalis, rosemary

Serissa foetida, serissa

---

eye. Topiary is a garden conceit, highly popular with the Romans and revived in the 16th and 17th centuries in European gardens, especially France and the Netherlands. Once the purview of the wealthy, topiaries have been democratized: Some of the most delightful examples in the U.S. are at Disneyland and Disneyworld.

Species with tight, slow growth and small foliage that can withstand constant and heavy pruning are ideal candidates for "topiarization" (see box, page 94). Some deciduous species are used for topiary, but if you live in a cold region, your pride and joy will be bare during the winter. Depending on the size and nature of your artistic conception—a to-scale botanical bovine, say—the project may require more than one plant.

Pick a plant that approximates the shape you want to create, *Taxus baccata* 'Columnaris' for an obelisk, for example, or *T.* × *media* 'Hatfieldii' for a green pyramid. Above all, make sure the plant is cold-hardy in your garden. If the peacock's fan is winterkilled, you may have to decapitate him as well and turn him into a Volkswagen bug.

You can attempt to turn a large shrub into a spaceship, but working with a young plant is usually easier than beginning with a mature one. Start when the plant is

Some Plants for Outdoor Topiary

Buxus microphylla var. *koreana*, Korean box

Buxus sempervirens, common box

Buxus sempervirens 'Suffructosa', dwarf box

Juniperus species, junipers

Ilex species, hollies

Picea glauca var. *albertiana*, Alberta spruce

Pyracantha coccinea, scarlet firethorn

Taxus baccata, English yew

Taxus × *media*, intermediate yew

Thuja species, arborvitaes

Tsuga canadensis, Canadian hemlock

small, and don't be overeager. Prune to encourage dense growth, aiming first for a basic shape, such as a cone, then begin making small cuts to create the figure you have in mind.

Once your hollies turn into a camel, they need only careful and diligent shaping and shearing to keep him trim and healthy. You must remove most of last year's growth, or your spiral or bird or table and chair will exceed its site. Pruning times vary according to the plant and the place. For big gaps and bare spots, prune in early spring, just before new growth begins.

Espalier

The French word *espalier* refers both to a plant grown in a pattern on a flat plane and to the vertical support, such as a wire, trellis, wall, or fence that it grows against. Like so many forms of fancy-pants gardening, espalier originated with the Romans. Many purely ornamental plants can be espaliered—pyracantha is a spectacular choice, as are camellias, flowering crabapples (*Malus*), witch hazels (*Hamamelis*), creeping fig (*Ficus pumila*), Pfitzer juniper (*Juniperus chinensis* 'Pfitzerana'), and flowering quince cultivars (*Chaenomeles*)—but apples (*Malus*), pears (*Pyrus*), cherries (*Prunus*), and other fruits are the classic quarry for this gorgeous form of botanical bondage. The best candidates have long, flexible branches, ornamental flowers or fruits, and good resistance to pests and diseases. Don't pick a shrub or tree that is significantly taller than the

Espalier Shapes

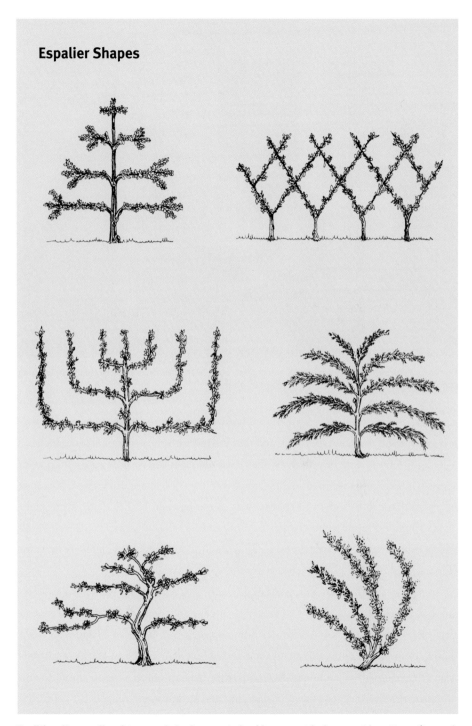

Traditionally, espaliered trees and shrubs were trained in symmetrical, geometric patterns (top and center). Today, more free-form designs are common (bottom). While space-saving and elegant, espalier requires a substantial commitment of time, especially during the training phase, and regular attention after the form has been established.

Firethorn, *Pyracantha,* can be grown as an espalier. Most of the intensive pruning this technique requires should be done while the plants are dormant in winter.

surface it will be growing against. If you want to espalier an apple or pear, make sure it is growing on dwarfing rootstock and that it fruits on spurs, short stubby branches.

In addition to being beautiful, espalier is a godsend if you're short on room: it saves space by making three-dimensional plants two dimensional, and it increases the range of plants that can be grown in cold regions. A gardener in USDA Zone 4 can plant 'Cox's Orange Pippin' apple, which is hardy only to USDA Zone 5, against a wall with a sunny exposure and plan on picking fruit for an apple pie. Gardeners in warm climates may need to give espaliers a less sunny exposure.

After choosing the plant you want to grow, the next decision is what design to create. Espaliered plants typically consist of a single main stem, the *leader,* and several tiers of horizontal or near-horizontal branches, or *arms.* You can invent your own design, but someone probably has beaten you to it. There are scores of classic patterns with romantic names such as palmette verrier, Belgian fence, Belgian doublet, and oblique palmette that have been challenging and delighting gardeners for centuries. Or you can be informal, following no clear pattern.

If you use a formal design, begin by erecting a strong form—wire is the usual material—that you want your espalier to follow. If you're planting against a solid surface like a wall, install the form at least six inches away from the wall to ensure good air circulation. You can either purchase a plant that has been pruned for espalier, one that is already growing on a trellis, or begin with an unpruned plant. Prune new plants sparingly until they are well established. (For details on pruning specific shrubs, trees, and vines, see the appropriate chapters in this book.)

Espalier involves training—forcing branches to grow in the direction you want—as well as pruning. Stems are most flexible when they are young, so don't wait too long to tie them to your support. Most pruning should be done when the espalier is dormant (or after it flowers, if it is a spring bloomer). Which stems you cut off and which you save depends on the pattern you've picked. Remove or redirect any stems that are heading either inward or outward, and always cut to buds or stems that are pointing in the direction you want the growth to go. If you've chosen a simple design, the basic framework may be established in three or four years; intricate designs take longer.

Just remember that with espaliers, growth must be directed, fastened, and curbed continually. The pruning and training never ends.

Pleaching

Pleaching, which comes from a word meaning *to braid*, involves weaving tree branches together to form living screens, arches and archways, lattices, arbors, pergolas, even houses. The technique has been around since the Romans, but its popularity ebbs and flows like the tides. Some of the best examples are at historic sites like Virginia's Colonial Williamsburg (see photo on page 89) and George Washington's home in Mount Vernon, but pleaching isn't something that should belong solely to the past. A pleached walkway covered by goldenchain trees (*Laburnum*) in full flower will have even the most outdoors-averse computer addict breathless with admiration.

All the plants in any pleaching project should be not only the same age and size but also the same species and/or cultivar. Likely candidates are trees with pliable branches, such as apples (*Malus*), willows (*Salix*), lindens (*Tilia*), hawthorns (*Crataegus*), beeches (*Fagus*), hornbeams (*Carpinus*), pears (*Pyrus*), and sycamores (or plane trees, *Platanus*). If you live in a tropical climate, bougainvilleas are sitting ducks for pleaching.

Classic pleaching involves making *grafting* cuts to ensure that plants literally grow together, or using plants that are inosculate, or graft naturally. Red maple and box-elder (*Acer rubrum*, *A. negundo*), beeches (*Fagus*), sycamores (*Platanus*), hornbeams (*Carpinus*), and lindens (*Tilia*) are among the trees known to inosculate. Grafting, natural or otherwise, isn't essential to pleaching, though. You can create the same effect simply by planting trees close together and encouraging lateral growth until their limbs intermingle. Tying stems together fosters natural grafting.

For screens and fences—which look like hedges on stilts—the pruning is similar to that involved in creating an espalier: turning three-dimensional plants into two-dimensional ones. For archways and arbors and tunnels, you may need to build a temporary framework of wood or wire on which to train the limbs. Once the branches weave together, the support can be removed. Remove any errant branches, and continue weaving shoots into the framework.

Pollarding

Pollarding is something you either love or hate. Also called *high coppicing,* it involves pruning a tree back to the trunk or a branch framework. Such severe cutting results in a flush of slender stems at the end of branches. Pollarding is a familiar practice in Europe, where it has traditionally been used to keep trees at a certain size—for example, the plane tree allées in southern France—and to create a formal look. However, pollarding is less seen and less admired on this side of the Atlantic, perhaps because trees used to have plenty of room to expand here. Lindens (*Tilia*), hornbeams (*Carpinus*), *Ginkgo,* beeches (*Fagus*), and *Catalpa* trees as well as plane trees (*Platanus*) and willows (*Salix*) are typical candidates for pollarding.

Pollarding

Pollarding keeps trees within bounds and creates a formal look. Branches can be trimmed all the way back to the trunk (A) or to a branch framework (B).

Coppicing has kept these willows (*Salix*) close to shrub size. It also produces an abundance of attractive, bright new stems. Used for ornamental effect here, willows have traditionally been coppiced for their crop of pliable young stems, which are harvested for use in basketry, fencing, trellises, and more.

To pollard back to the main stem, select a tree with a clear stem about six feet high or the desired height for the pollarded head. Begin by pruning back all the branches to the main stem in late winter or early spring; in the case of trees with many branches, this pruning is best carried out over two to three years to reduce stressing the plant. Continue pruning out new growth every other year until a swollen head is established, then every year or every other year thereafter. When new branch growth becomes congested, thin it out. To create a pollard with a branch framework, choose a well-branched tree. Prune back dormant branches to three to six feet from the trunk in late winter or early spring. Prune as described above to establish pollarded heads at each branch tip.

Coppicing refers to the same drastic pruning technique when it's done close to the ground. In ornamental gardening, coppicing is popular for shrubs with colorful stems like *Kerria japonica* and red osier and Tartarian dogwoods (*Cornus stolonifera, C. alba*), which are cut to the ground each spring to produce an abundance of colorful new stems. (See the photo on page 13.)

Outfitting the Pruner: Tools and Equipment

If you ever doubted that English writer Vita Sackville-West was a real gardener, all suspicions will disappear after reading these lines from her long poem "The Garden" (1946):

> Whether the twiggy hornbeam or the beech,
> The quick, the holly, or the lime to pleach
> Or little box, or gravity of yew
> Cut into battlements to frame a view
> Before the frost can harm the wounded tips
> Throughout the days he trims and clips and snips
> As must the guardian of the child correct
> Distorted growth and tendencies to wrong,
> Suppress the weakness, countenance the strong...

Now that's a writer who knew the difference between anvil and bypass secateurs, the high-hat name for pruning shears. Hers probably came from a firm with an appointment to the House of Windsor.

Royal appointment or no royal appointment, you don't want to scrimp on the quality either. Well-made cutting tools are never a waste of money, and there are plenty of good makers. ARS, Corona, Felco, Fiskars, and Sandvik are five names to look for. Even Stihl, famous for chain saws, has gotten into the business. If possible, try a tool before you open your wallet. Is it too heavy? Does it feel too light? And don't just

The two hand pruners on the left can cut through stems up to half an inch in diameter. They are the type of pruning tool you'll need most often. The two flower shears on the right cut soft, delicate stems.

hold it: Use it. Is it easy to operate? Does it cut smoothly? Can it handle the size cuts you need to make?

If you choose carefully, you won't end up with a collection of pruning equipment you never use. In truth, most of us need little more than a good pair of pruning shears and a pruning saw—although plenty more tools are available. Unless you have an especially good garden store nearby, shop by mail or online in order to take advantage of the astonishing array of what's for sale—not just different tools but different models, grades, and sizes. And better prices.

Prices vary enormously—as much as 50 percent—so compare before you buy. (Try using one of the online price-comparison search engines, such as www.dealtime.com. The prices listed below are from mail-order or online sites.) And if you discover a tool looked better in the picture than it feels in your hand, send it back. Most firms are understanding about returns.

Two kinds of hand pruners: The one on the left has bypass blades, the one on the right has an anvil blade.

For top quality, look for terms like "professional," "classic," or "heavy duty." Unless you prune only every other year, investing in a "pro" model is money saved in the long run. If possible, opt for tools that come with lifetime warranties, which more and more manufacturers now offer.

Pruners, Loppers, and More

Hand tools that cut, not saw, are the pruning tools you'll use most often. There is a gaggle of choices, ranging from tools for big jobs to tools for small cuts. You don't need everything, but probably you will want more than one.

Hand Pruners If there is a single, indispensable tool for pruning, it's a pair of hand shears, or hand pruners. Flower gardeners opt for flower shears, scissorlike cutters designed for snipping soft stems. You'll need something more substantial for pruning trees, shrubs, and vines, pruners that will cut woody stems up to at least half an inch in diameter.

Eliminate any pruners that don't have blades made from high-tempered carbon steel, which can be sharpened. It's also important that you can replace blades and springs. You won't be able to repair—or replace parts—on pruners put together with rivets, so look for nuts and bolts.

Quality manufacturers sell hand pruners in left- as well as right-handed models. And if you wear a belt, think about getting a leather scabbard so that you don't lose your pruners ($15). Last, sharp tools make cleaner cuts and require less effort on your part. A pocket-sized sharpening stone is enough to keep cutting tools sharp ($5).

The basic choice in pruners is design: bypass or anvil. Bypass pruners have one curved blade—sharpened on its outside edge—that slips past a thicker unsharpened hook. They make close, neat cuts and are the overwhelming favorite of most gardeners. The gold standard for bypass pruners is the Felco #2, which professionals have sworn by for more than four decades. Superb in

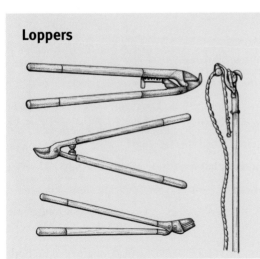

Loppers

On the left, from top to bottom: ratchet lopper, bypass lopper, and anvil lopper. Right: pole pruner.

Loppers are long-handled pruners meant for branches that are up to two inches thick. They are useful to prune hard-to-reach branches as well as prickly stems.

design, materials, and quality, this pruner from Switzerland has replaceable parts, padded alloy handles, rubber cushion shock absorber, sap groove, even a notch to cut wire ($35 to $50). For smaller hands, look for Felco #6, a down-sized version of #2 that is smaller but not less expensive.

There are other good pruners from other good companies. If your hands tire quickly, consider ergonomically designed models. Some come with a rotating handle that reduces the power you have to put into a cut. Fiskars #7936 is one choice; it has Xylan®-coated blades and polycarbonate handles, and is both strong and lightweight ($30 to $50). There are self-oiling models, pruners that discharge a disinfectant as they cut, even electronic and pneumatic pruners. As gardeners stocked with dozens of tools that they never use have learned to say, "Don't go there."

Rosarians may want to look into cut-and-hold pruners, models that hang on to stems after they're cut. ARS and Corona are among the firms that make them ($35 to $50). There are also hand pruners designed to use with two hands. Don't be tempted. If a stem is big enough for two hands, you need loppers or a saw. And you're unlikely to be happy with telescopic- or long-handled pruners. They have bypass blades mounted at the end of a lightweight pole, two to four feet long. Nice idea, but your hand will tire hours before your pruning is completed.

Anvil pruners are the second choice. They have a cutting blade sharpened on both sides that closes against an anvil, a flat brass or fiberglass-reinforced nylon blade. It's like using a kitchen knife against a cutting board. Anvil pruners are better for big, tough cuts—superior for taking out dead wood—but they tend to crush stems rather than slice them, and you can't snuggle in for really close cuts.

Anvil pruners tend to be less expensive than their bypass cousins, running anywhere from $15 to $50 depending on quality. Top of the line is the Felco #30 ($35). A nice variation on anvil pruners are ratchet-cut models, which are geared to make large cuts easy. The original was—and still is—the yellow-handled Florian #701 that claims to multiply "your strength up to 700 percent" ($38). Fiskars and C.K. also make ratchet-action pruners.

Lopping Pruners Think of loppers as pruning shears on a stick. Heavy-duty pruning shears on two sticks, actually. It's those long handles that allow you to reach beyond arm's length and to cut much larger branches—from one to two inches— than hand pruners could manage. Like hand pruners, though, loppers are either bypass or anvil. There also are ratcheting models to give you more leverage on really big stems. Whatever the style, be sure yours have replaceable carbon-steel blades, rubber cushions, or bumpers, to minimize shock, and comfortable grips.

More and more loppers come with lightweight tubular steel, aluminum, or fiberglass handles fitted with cushioned grips, but there's nothing wrong with the traditional wood. Handles in the 15- to 24-inch range are light enough for most gardeners to manage; longer-handled loppers are heavier and less easy to control, but they give you better reach and more power.

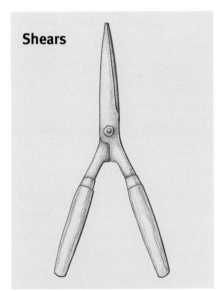

Shears

Hand hedge shears have blades that are between 8 and 12 inches long.

Loppers aren't cheap. Top-of-the-line models from Felco, Hickok, Sandvik, Snap Cut, and other good makers cost between $60 and $125. Models with special features, such as the Florian ratchet lopper, will set you back nearly $200. That's a lot of money for a tool you won't use every week. For cuts that pruning shears can't handle, most gardeners are better off with a small pruning saw.

Pole Pruners Pole pruners are also pruning shears on a stick, one long stick. Heavy-

The holly, *Ilex*, is being pruned with hand hedge shears, which can cut through branches up to a quarter-inch thick.

duty models, the kind the power companies use, are overkill for most home gardeners. Standard-size models cut limbs up to two inches in diameter. (You make the cut by pulling on a rope or a sliding collar that is connected by a gear to the bypass blades.) Most models—made by Fiskars, Snap Cut, Corona, and others—have lightweight telescoping fiberglass poles that extend to 12 feet. Many also come with a small saw mounted just above the pruner blades, for branches larger than the pruner can handle ($60 to $125).

A first-rate tool for home gardeners who don't need to reach sky-high is Fiskars' "Pruning Stik." It's 62 inches long—giving you about a ten-foot reach—and weighs less than two pounds. Its rotating head secures close cuts, up to 1½ inches. And it's not just for overhead: Many gardeners use it with thorny plants, even low-growing plants when they don't want to kneel ($65).

Hedge Shears Purists may swear by hand models, but most homeowners have converted to electric- or gasoline-powered hedge shears. The type and size of your hedge—and your energy—should dictate the power source. If you're maintaining a boundless formal hedge, power equipment makes sense. But if your hedge is small or informal, a mixture of deciduous and/or evergreen species, you won't need anything more that a traditional pair of hedge shears. Hedge shears are designed for pruning hedges, not general pruning chores. (Similarly, chain saws are for cutting wood, not shearing hedges.)

Hand hedge shears are like two-handed scissors with blades measuring between 8 and 12 inches long that can cut stems up to a quarter of an inch in diameter. Most have long ash or fiberglass handles and come with a notch on one blade for cutting large stems. Look for shears with carbon-steel blades, rubber bumpers to absorb the shock when you cut, and for models with an adjustable locknut at the hinge, which will allow you to adjust the tension. Hedge shears with wavy or serrated blades are designed to hold branches as you cut, but they tend to cut less cleanly than straight-edged models. Professional-grade models from firms such as ARS and Corona cost $45 to $85.

Power hedge shears, either electric or gasoline, look like the front end of a swordfish. Equipped with moving teeth, they cut quickly and with minimal effort on the gardener's part. At the same time, they don't cut as cleanly as hand shears, they tend to jam if they encounter large stems, and they are noisy. Remember, too, that it's easy to make mistakes with power hedge shears, and that they can cut the pruner as efficiently as they cut his or her hedge.

Power hedge shears are useful for maintaining a large formal hedge, but they don't cut as cleanly as hand hedge shears.

A pruning saw with a tri-cut blade is the tool to use for cutting through limbs that are up to ten inches across. A pruning saw cuts on the pull stroke, which makes it easy to use.

Knives A knife is not an essential pruning tool, although it's handy to have one in your pocket. *Pruning knives,* most of which have small hooked blades and gorgeous handles made from some exotic wood, may be "lightweight, sturdy, and handsome," as the Berger Bilhook pruning knife advertises itself, but most home pruners don't need one ($20 to $70).

Saws The carpenter's saw you use to cut two-by-fours is not the saw to take into the garden. You need a *pruning saw,* one designed not to gum up and bind when you cut live wood. The most versatile pruning saws—sometimes called *orchard* or *tree saws*—have either straight or tapered curved blades, 12 to 16 inches long, and are fitted with a pistol or modified pistol (banana) grip. They cut on the pull stroke and can slice through limbs up to ten inches across. No homeowner should be without a pruning saw, and *no pruning saw should be without a tri-cut blade.*

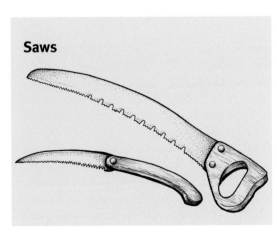

Saws

A pruning saw with a tri-cut blade and a folding pruning saw with the same type of blade. You will need a saw for most branches greater than two inches in diameter.

The tri-cut saw masquerades under other names—*turbo-cut, Japanese, razor-tooth, power-tooth,* or *three-cut saw*—but whatever the name, be sure it's what you buy. After one cut, you'll know that all other pruning saws, beginning with the copper models made by the Egyptians 6,000 years ago, are also-rans. Its secret is in its teeth. Rather than the standard two sharpened edges, the tri-cut has three: one on each side of the pyramidal tooth, which is angled straight up from the blade, and a third edge on the tooth's point. When you pull the saw toward yourself, the point edge digs into the limb while the side edges cut it.

Hand Pruners

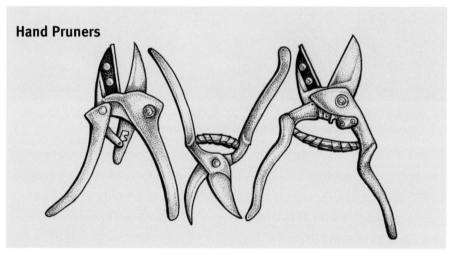

From left to right: Anvil pruner with ratchets, bypass pruner, and regular anvil pruner. Look for a model assembled with screws and bolts, so you can replace blades and springs as needed.

Tool Tune-Ups

"Give me six hours to chop down a tree and I will spend the first four sharpening the axe." Abraham Lincoln, America's most famous rail-splitter, said that. Axes aren't for pruning, but Lincoln's wisdom is applicable to true pruning tools. For shears and loppers, use a wet sharpening stone frequently to keep the cutting blade keen. Sharpen only the side or sides of blades that have already been sharpened, and sharpen at the same angle. Anvil pruners should be sharpened on both sides of one blade—be sure your sharpening doesn't put a curve on the blade, which needs to be flat. Sharpen bypass and hedge pruners and bypass loppers on the outside edge of both blades. Keep your pruners clean—remove any sap or pitch with a solvent like paint thinner—and use oil to lubricate the pivot and keep the metal protected against rust. Clean saw blades regularly with a solvent and oil them to prevent rusting. Sharpening pruning saws requires a special file and a patient sharpener; you're better off taking this job to an expert. Sand wood handles if necessary, then treat with linseed oil.

Tri-cut blades stay sharp longer than traditional blades and can be sharpened (there is a sharpener designed for tri-cut saws, $15). Sharpening saws is no picnic, though, so pick a model with a replaceable blade ($12 to $25). A cushioned handle is more comfortable—and more expensive—but a wood handle works fine. Saw prices run $20 to $55, depending on quality and blade length (13 inches is a good size for general use). Like pruning shears, pruning saws are available in different grades; look for words such as "professional" and "heavy duty" for saws that will hold up to hard use. Don't even consider a saw with a conventional blade.

A *folding pruning saw* is the saw equivalent of the "lady's spade" and just as useful. The smallest models are less than nine inches long folded, diminutive enough for a pocket. Designed to cut branches up to four inches, the best models, such as the Felco #60, have locking devices to keep the blade from opening or shutting unexpectedly. With tri-cut blades, they run $15 to $40.

Raker, or *coarse-tooth, saws* are for big cuts up to 20 inches in diameter. They have D-shaped handles and blades from 20 to 26 inches long. You're unlikely to need a saw this big; if you do, make sure it has a tri-cut blade ($50).

Pole saws are just what their name implies: a saw mounted on the top of a pole. Occasionally useful, they do keep gardeners off tall ladders and can handle limbs larger than a pole pruner can. But they aren't all that easy to use and don't come cheap: Blades (13 inches) alone run about $50, and a telescoping pole with an 18-foot reach is another $200. For serious pruners only. (Another way to keep your feet on the ground while removing a high limb is to use a rope saw, a blade with ropes attached to both ends [$45]. Sounds simple. Isn't simple. Take a pass.)

Box saws are picturesque but they are made for the woodpile, not pruning. Don't let their inexpensive price tempt you. Chain saws are beyond the scope of this book except to say that they're loud, polluting, and extremely dangerous.

For More Information

The American Horticultural Society Pruning & Training
Christopher D. Brickell and
David Joyce
DK Publishing, 1996

Easy-Care Roses
Stephen Scanniello, editor
Brooklyn Botanic Garden, 1995

The Graham Stuart Thomas Rose Book
G.S. Thomas
Timber Press, 1994

Growing Roses in Cold Climates
Jerry Olson and John Whitman
Contemporary Books, 1998

Manual of Woody Landscape Plants
Michael A. Dirr
Stipes Publishing, 1998

Modern Arboriculture
Alex L. Shigo
Shigo and Trees, Associates, 1991

100 Tree Myths
Alex L. Shigo
Shigo and Trees, Associates, 1993

The Pruning Book
Lee Reich
Taunton Press, 1997

The Pruning of Trees, Shrubs and Conifers
George E. Brown
Timber Press, 1972

Roses of America
Stephen Scanniello
Henry Holt, 1990

Tree Basics
Alex L. Shigo
Shigo and Trees, Associates, 1996

Tree Pruning
Alex L. Shigo
Shigo and Trees, Associates, 1989

Organizations and Suppliers

Organizations

The web sites of the arborist organizations include databases of certified arborists qualified to perform professional tree consulting and maintenance. You can search the sites by zip code or state.

American Society of Consulting Arborists
15245 Shady Grove Road, Suite 130
Rockville, MD 20850
301-947-0483
www.asca-consultants.org

International Society of Arboriculture
P.O. Box 3129
Champaign, IL 61826
217-355-9411
www.isa-arbor.com

Tree Care Industry Association
(formerly National Arborist Association)
3 Perimeter Road, Unit 1
Manchester, NH 03103
800-733-2622
www.natlarb.com

Tool Suppliers

A.M. Leonard
241 Fox Drive
Piqua, OH 45356
800-543-8955
www.amleo.com

The Eclectic Gardener
5227 Dredger Way
Orangevale, CA 95662
916-987-7490
http://store.yahoo.com/eclectic-gardener

Gempler's, Inc.
100 Countryside Drive
Belleville, WI 53508
800-332-6744
www.gemplers.com

Harmony Farm Supply
3244 Highway 16 North
Sebastopol, CA 95472
707-823-9125
www.harmonyfarm.com

Lee Valley Tools Ltd.
P.O. Box 1780
Ogdensburg, NY 13669
800-871-8158
www.leevalley.com

Little's Good Gloves
P.O. Box 1966
Sedona, AZ 86339
888-967-5548
www.mudglove.com

OESCO, Inc.
P.O. Box 540
Conway, MA 01341
800-634-5557
www.oescoinc.com

Orchard's Edge
836 Arlington Heights Road #233
Elk Grove Village, IL 60007
877-881-1426
www.orchardsedge.com

Peaceful Valley Farm Supply
P.O. Box 2209
Grass Valley, CA 95945
888-784-1722
www.groworganic.com

M.K. Rittenhouse & Sons
RR 3, 1402 4th Avenue
St. Catharines, ON, L2R 6P9, Canada
877-488-1914
www.rittenhouse.ca

Samia Rose Topiary
1236 Urania Avenue
Encinitas, CA 92023
800-488-6742
www.srtopiary.com

Contributors

KARAN DAVIS CUTLER, who has edited five previous BBG handbooks—*Essential Tools, Salad Gardens, Tantalizing Tomatoes, Flowering Vines,* and *Starting from Seed*—gardens on 15 acres in northern Vermont. A frequent contributor to national garden magazines, her latest book is *The New England Gardener's Book of Lists* (2000).

Thanks go to Brooklyn Botanic Garden rosarian **ANNE O'NEILL** for her editorial advice.

Illustrations

PAUL HARWOOD pages 20, 27, 35, 59, 70, 81

STEPHEN K-M. TIM pages 21, 46, 61, 90, 92, 95, 98

EMMA SKURNICK pages 102, 104, 107, 108

Photos

HELENA FIERLINGER cover

DAVID CAVAGNARO pages 2, 29 both, 33 right, 56, 65, 69 right, 75, 76, 79, 83, 90

JERRY PAVIA pages 4, 9 left, 13, 23 left, 32, 36, 55, 73, 85, 86, 94, 96

WALTER CHANDOHA pages 6, 8, 15, 16, 18, 20 both, 40, 42, 43, 45 left

DEREK FELL pages 9 right, 31, 48, 103, 105, 106, 107

NEIL SODERSTROM pages 10 both, 24 all, 25, 33 left, 101 both

CHRIS RODDICK page 22

ALAN & LINDA DETRICK pages 23 right, 45 right, 54, 66, 67, 69 left, 70, 80, 82

GEORGE AVERY page 47 all

KAREN BUSSOLINI page 89 (Governor's Palace, Colonial Williamsburg, VA), 99

Index

A

Abelia × *grandiflora*
(Glossy), 32
Abies, 60, 62
Abutilon, 32
Acer, 16, 20, 39, 51
negundo, 98
palmatum, 49
rubrum, 8, 44, 45, 98
Actinidia, 71
Aesculus
hippocastanum, 45
parviflora, 32
Albizia julibrissin, 16, 52
Allspice, Carolina, 33
Almond, Flowering, 37–38
Althea, Shrub, 35
Amelanchier, 32, 39
× *grandiflora*, 52
Anvil pruners, 103–104, 108
Apical dominance, 14, 44, 57
Apple, 17, 46, 96, 97
Aralia, Five-Leaf, 30, 34
Araucaria heterophylla, 17
Arborvitae, 13, 54, 56, 57, 58,
61, 64, 88, 94
Eastern, 11
Arbutus unedo, 32
Aristolochia macrophylla, 71
Aronia arbutifolia, 32
Artemisia, 33

Ash, 51
Mountain, 17, 53
Austin, David, 82
Azalea, 38

B

Bald Cypress, 56, 64
Bamboo, Yellow Grove, 28
Bamboo Hedge, 9
Bay, Sweet, 28
Bay Star Vine, 73
Beautyberry, 33
Beautybush, 30, 36
Beech, 51, 98, 99
American, 23
European, 44, 45
Betula, 16, 21, 51
nigra, 50
pendula, 45
Bignonia capreolata, 71
Birch, 16, 21, 51
European White, 45
River, 50
Bittersweet, 68, 71
Oriental, 71, 75
Black Haw, 39
Bonsai, 10, 88
Boston Ivy, 7, 9, 73
Bougainvillea, 71, 93
Box-Elder, 98
Box saw, 109

Boxwood, 22, 88
Common, 94
English, 30, 33
Korean, 94
Branch bark ridge, 26, 47
Branch collar, 25, 47, 59
Bridalwreath, 38
Buckeye, Bottlebrush, 32
Buddleja
alternifolia, 33
globosa, 28
Buds
heading cuts, 20, 21, 25
latent, 58
lateral, 14, 44
terminal (apical), 14, 43–44
water sprouts at, 47–48
Butterfly Bush, Fountain, 33
Buxus, 22, 88
microphylla, 94
sempervirens, 30, 33, 94
Bypass pruners, 102–103,
104, 108

C

Callicarpa, 33
Calluna vulgaris, 33
Calycanthus floridus, 33
Camellia, 16, 93, 94
japonica, 33, 39
Campsis radicans, 71

Candling, 60, 61
Canopy
    cleaning, 50
    raising, 51
    thinning, 50
Carbohydrate-nitrogen
    balance, 14
Carpinus, 51, 90, 98, 99
Carya
    illinoinensis, 49
    ovata, 44
Catalpa, 99
    bignonioides (Southern), 52
Cedar, 13, 57, 62
    Red, 62–63, 88
    Swamp, 64
    White, 62, 64
Cedrus, 62
Celastrus
    orbiculatus, 71, 75
    scandens, 68, 71
Cercis canadensis, 51, 52
Chaenomeles, 33, 88, 94
Chamaecyparis, 56, 62
Chaste Tree, 39, 53
Cherry, 94
    Flowering, 37–38, 53
Chimonanthus praecox, 34
Chimonobambusa marmorea, 9
Chionanthus virginicus, 52
Chokeberry, 32
Cinquefoil, 88
    Bush, 30, 37
Cladrastis lutea, 52
Clematis, 8, 17, 20, 74
Clethra alnifolia, 8, 30, 34
Cocculus carolinus, 72
Colette, 7
Conifers, 54–64
    growth habits of, 57
    hedge plants, 88, 90
    overgrown, 54
    shapes and sizes, 54, 56
Conifers, pruning
    hedges, 63, 91
    maintenance, 17

mature conifers, 61–62
plant-by-plant guide, 62–64
shrubs, 57
techniques, 58–60
young conifers, 60–61
Coral Beads, 72
Coralberry, 38
Cornus, 52
    alba, 12
    alternifolia, 39, 45
    florida, 51
    kousa, 51
    stolonifera, 12, 34
Corylopsis, 34, 39
Corylus
    avellana, 39
    avellana 'Contorta', 52
    maxima, 13
Cotinus coggygria, 34, 39
Cow-Itch, 71
Crabapple, 9, 16, 17, 46,
    53, 94
Cranberry Bush
    American, 12, 15–16, 39
    European, 24
Crape Myrtle, 16, 36, 39,
    51, 52
Crataegus, 46, 52, 88, 98
    crus-galli, 51
    phaenopyrum, 44
Crossvine, 71
Crown raising/thinning, 23
Cupressus, 57, 62
Currant, Alpine, 88
Cuts. *See* Pruning
    techniques
Cypress, 57, 62
    Bald, 56, 64
    False, 56, 57, 62

D
Daphne, 30, 34
Date, Chinese, 53
Deadheading, 80, 86
Deutzia, 34
Diseased plants, 26

Dogwood, 52
    Kousa, 51
    Pagoda, 39, 45
    Red Osier, 12, 34
    Tartarian, 12
Douglas Fir, 63
Drop crotching, 50–51
Dutchman's pipe, 71

E
Eleutherococcus
    sieboldianus, 30, 34
Ellis, Barbara, 22
Elm, 50
Epicormic shoots, 11
Ergonomic tools, 109
Erica, 34
Espalier, 94–97
Evergreens. *See* Conifers

F
Fagus, 51, 98, 99
    grandifolia, 23
    sylvatica, 44, 45
Fall pruning, 16
False Cypress, 56, 57, 62
Fastigiate trees, 44
Ficus pumila, 72, 94
Fig, Creeping/Climbing, 72, 94
Filbert
    European, 39
    Purple-Leafed, 13
Fir, 54, 57, 60, 62
    Douglas Fir, 63
Fire blight, 17, 46
Firethorn, 38, 94
Flowering, pruning for, 12–13,
    21–22
Flowers and Fruit
    (Colette), 7
Forsythia, 12, 16, 30, 34
Fothergilla, 34, 88
Franklinia alatamaha, 51, 52
Franklin Tree, 51, 52
Fraxinus, 51
Fringe Tree, White, 52

Frost, Robert, 57
Fruiting, pruning for, 12–13,
    21–22

G
Gardenia, 93
    augusta (Common), 30, 34
"Garden, The" (Sackville-
    West, Vita), 100
Gelsemium sempervirens, 72
Ginkgo, 99
Girdle, tree, 43
Golden Bell, 34
Goldenrain Tree, 16, 51, 52
Grafting cuts, 98
Grape, 68, 74
    Oregon, 37
Grape Holly, 37
Growth
    apical dominance and, 14,
    43–44
hard pruning and, 12, 14, 78
    pruning to limit, 11–12, 28
Gum, Sweet, 44, 45

H
Hackmatack, 63
Halesia tetraptera, 52
Hamamelis, 35, 39, 94
Handbook for Selecting
    Roses, 81
Hand pruners, 25,
    102–104, 108
Harry Lauder's Walking Stick, 52
Hat racking, 22
Hawthorn, 46, 52, 88, 97–98
    Cockspur, 51
    Washington, 44
Hazel
    Winter, 34, 39
    Witch, 35, 39
Heading cuts, 20–22, 25, 31, 47
Health, pruning for, 11, 16–17
Heather, 34
    Scotch, 33
Hedges, 16, 22

conifer, 63, 88, 89
    formal, 90, 91
    informal, 90–91
    plant selection, 88, 90
    radical pruning, 91
Hedge shears, 91, 105–106
Hemlock, 57, 58, 64, 88
    Canadian, 94
    Weeping, 62
Hibiscus syriacus, 30, 35, 39
Hickory, Shagbark, 44
Hill, Lewis, 91
Holly, 30, 35, 39, 90, 94
Honeysuckle, 68, 69
    Henry's, 72
    Japanese, 72, 75
    Trumpet, 72
Hop, Common, 72
Hornbeam, 51, 90, 98, 99
Horsechestnut, 45
Hoya carnosa, 68
Humulus lupulus, 72
Hydrangea
    aborescens (Hills-of-
    Snow), 35
    paniculata (Peegee), 35
    petiolaris (Climbing), 8, 72
    quercifolia (Oak-Leaf), 35
    Hydrangea Vine, 74

I
Ice removal, 51
Ilex, 30, 35, 39, 90, 94
    verticillata, 12, 30, 35
Internodes, 14
Invasive plants
    shrubs, 37
    trees, 53
    vines, 75
Ipomoea, 72
Itea virginica, 30, 35, 88
Ivy, Boston, 7, 9, 73

J
Jasmine, 69
    invasive, 75

Poet's (Common), 72
    Primrose, 72
    Winter, 72
Jasminum, 69
    azoricum, 75
    dichotomum, 75
    mesnyi, 72
    nudiflorum, 72
    officinale, 72
Jessamine, Carolina, 72
Joyce, David, 10
Jujuba, Chinese, 53
Juneberry, 32
Juniper, 13, 56, 57, 58,
    62–63, 94
    Creeping (*horizontalis*), 58
    Pfitzer (*J. chinensis*
    'Pfitzerana'), 94
    Rocky Mountain
    (*J. virginiana*), 88

K
Kalmia latifolia, 24, 35–36, 90
Kerria japonica, 12, 36
Kiwi Vine, 71
Knives, pruning, 107
Koelreuteria paniculata, 16,
    51, 52
Kolkwitzia amabilis, 30, 36

L
Lagerstroemia indica, 16, 36,
    39, 51, 52
Larch, 56, 63
Larix, 63
    decidua, 56
Laurel, Bay, 93
Laurus nobilis, 93
Lifting, 61
Lilac, 15–16, 20, 26, 30,
    38–39, 88
    Japanese Tree, 8, 53
Lily-of-the-Valley Tree, 53
Limb removal, 46
Linden, 51, 97, 98, 99
Lindera benzoin, 36